One Billion Buyers

Strategies for Global Market Reach

COPYRIGHT NOTICE

Limits of Liability / Disclaimer

Table of Contents

Introduction

In a world where the lines of commerce are constantly shifting, the global market isn't just a huge sea of chances; it's more like a colorful quilt stitched together from various cultures, traditions, and shopping habits. Thanks to the internet, the way businesses connect with customers has totally changed. Those barriers that used to keep local shops from competing with big international brands? Yeah, they've pretty much crumbled. Nowadays, a small artisan selling handmade crafts in a busy local market can reach a million potential buyers on the other side of the planet with just a simple click. But here's the million-dollar question: how do you navigate this tangled web of global commerce? How do businesses make genuine connections with folks who speak different languages, celebrate different holidays, and have totally different values?

The key is diving deep into the nuances of global markets. It's not just about slapping a product on a shelf and hoping for the best; it's about building real connections that resonate with customers on a personal level. This journey starts with understanding the unique buying habits that vary from region to region, which highlights the importance of cultural sensitivity and local know-how. When businesses step into new markets, they've got to be flexible not just in their marketing but in what they're actually offering. It's all about making sure their products reflect the tastes and preferences of the people they're trying to reach.

In today's e-commerce age, where online shopping feels as natural as breathing for millions, the potential for growth is absolutely limitless. Social media has turned into a powerhouse for businesses, changing how they connect with consumers. Influencers have become the new trendsetters, swaying buying decisions with just a post or a story. Plus, the direct interactions on these platforms can build brand loyalty that knows no borders. But, with this power comes a big responsibility. Companies need to be aware of their impact, embracing sustainable practices that really resonate with today's eco-conscious shoppers.

Listening to customers has never been more vital. Feedback isn't just a nice-to-have; it's like a treasure map leading to success. By genuinely engaging with their audience, businesses can fine-tune their products and services, turning complaints into stepping stones for growth. A strong brand isn't just about being recognized; it's about building trust, reliability, and keeping promises. As companies carve out their identities, they need to create consistent messaging that speaks to the hearts of their customers, fostering a loyal following that champions their mission.

When it comes to marketing strategies, they're the lifeblood of any successful venture. Understanding the ins and outs of target demographics and using creative techniques can make a world of difference in grabbing attention and boosting sales. And as logistics and supply chains keep evolving, being able to deliver products efficiently is more important than ever. In a world where everyone wants things right now, businesses have to ensure that their customers get what they want, when they want it.

Technology is a game-changer in this ever-evolving landscape. From data analytics that reveal buying patterns to cool innovations like virtual reality that enhance customer experiences, the right tech can launch businesses to new heights. But with all this power comes a fair bit of complexity. Navigating the regulations that govern international trade is crucial to avoid pitfalls and stay compliant. Understanding trade agreements can open up new markets, giving you a competitive edge in a crowded field.

Looking ahead, the global commerce scene is bursting with possibilities. Emerging technologies like artificial intelligence and blockchain are transforming how we do business, offering insights and efficiencies that once seemed like science fiction. Staying on top of economic trends and adapting to changing consumer demands will be essential for anyone looking to thrive in this dynamic environment.

This book is your roadmap through the intricate maze of global markets. It's an invitation to explore strategies that can take your business from local to global, empowering you to connect with a billion potential buyers. As you flip through these pages, get ready to uncover the secrets of successful international commerce, where each chapter reveals new insights and opportunities. The world is waiting for you are you ready to grab your piece of the pie?

Chapter 1

Understanding Global Markets

Ever stepped into a store and felt like you've been transported to another universe? It's mind-boggling how different countries have their own distinct buying habits. What's a hot seller in one corner of the globe might just sit there collecting dust in another. You see, understanding these cultural quirks is crucial for cracking the code of global markets. Think of it as piecing together a jigsaw puzzle where every piece has its own unique shape and color.

Let's dig deeper. Each country has its own rhythm, right? The way people shop is shaped by their culture, traditions, and even their economic landscape. Take Japan, for instance. The convenience store culture is off the charts seriously, you can find everything from sushi to socks at 3 AM. Meanwhile, in the U.S., we're all about those sprawling big-box stores, where you can grab a gallon of milk and a flat-screen TV in one fell swoop. It's all about what feels familiar and comfortable for the locals.

So, what does this mean for you? If you're aiming to sell products on a global scale, you've got to roll up your sleeves and do some serious homework. You can't just slap a price tag on something and cross your fingers. No way, José! You need to dive headfirst into understanding local preferences. What snacks are all the rage in Brazil? What's trending in South Korea?

Here's a little nugget of wisdom: connect with local experts or even hire a consultant who knows the ins and outs of the market. They can provide insights that'll save you from making rookie mistakes. It's like having a cheat sheet for the final exam of global selling.

Now, let's chat about the internet. Ah, the magical world wide web! It's like a superhighway that's made it easier than ever for businesses to reach customers across the globe. Remember the days when you had to rely on snail mail and print ads? Yikes! Now, with just a few clicks, you can showcase your products to a billion potential buyers.

But here's the kicker: just because you can reach them doesn't mean you will. You need to tailor your online presence to fit different markets. Think about it what works in your backyard might not resonate with someone halfway across the world. Your website should reflect local languages, currencies, and even payment methods.

You want to connect with your audience, right? So, speak their language literally! If you're targeting customers in France, you better have a website that's not just translated but localized. That means understanding idioms, cultural references, and even humor. You don't want to accidentally offend someone with a poorly translated tagline. That'd be like trying to sell ice to an Eskimo just doesn't make sense!

Now, let's not forget about the importance of local languages and cultures. This is where the magic really happens. When you take the time to understand and respect local customs, you're not just selling a product; you're building a relationship. It's like making a new friend you wouldn't show up at their door without knowing a thing about them, right?

Imagine strolling into a market in Mexico and greeting the vendor in Spanish. The smile on their face? Priceless! You've just established a connection that transcends the mere transaction. They're far more likely to trust you and make a purchase. That's the power of cultural understanding.

So, how do you get started? First off, do some research; Look into the cultural norms and buying behaviors of your target market. Are there specific holidays when people splurge? What values do they hold dear? Once you have that info, you can tailor your marketing strategy to fit their lifestyle.

Here's a practical exercise: pick a country you're interested in and spend an hour researching their shopping habits. What do they value? How do they prefer to shop? Write down your findings and see how you can apply that to your business.

In the end, understanding global markets isn't just about crunching numbers and analyzing stats. It's about connecting with people. It's about grasping their needs and desires. The internet has opened up a world of possibilities, but it's up to you to navigate it wisely.

So, what's the takeaway here? Be adaptable. Be curious. And most importantly, be respectful of the cultures you're engaging with. You'll not only expand your reach but also create a loyal customer base that feels valued and understood.

Now, let's roll up our sleeves and make some global waves!

The Puzzle of Cultural Nuances

Let's face it: cultural nuances can feel like a foreign language, even if you're fluent in the local lingo. Each culture has its own set of unwritten rules, and navigating these can be as tricky as walking a tightrope. But fear not! Understanding these subtleties can be your secret weapon in the global marketplace.

Think about it: how often have you heard a joke that just didn't land because it was too steeped in cultural references? You want your marketing to resonate, not leave your audience scratching their heads. When you're aware of cultural nuances, you can craft messages that hit home.

For example, let's talk about colors. In some cultures, white symbolizes purity and peace, while in others, it's associated with mourning. If you're launching a product that features a prominent color, you better know what it signifies in your target market. A misstep here could cost you sales or worse, create a PR nightmare.

Food is another area where cultural understanding pays off. If you're marketing snacks, for instance, consider local tastes and preferences. What's considered a delicacy in one country might be viewed with skepticism in another. When KFC launched in India, they had to adapt their menu to cater to local tastes hello, vegetarian options!

The key takeaway? Do your research and be open to learning. This isn't just about selling; it's about fostering connections. When you respect and embrace cultural differences, you're not just a seller; you're a partner in their consumer journey.

Digital Strategies for Global Engagement

Now that we've tackled the cultural side of things, let's pivot to the digital realm. The internet is a game-changer for global marketing, but it's not a one-size-fits-all solution. You've got to strategize to ensure your online presence resonates with diverse audiences.

Start with your website. It's your digital storefront, and first impressions matter. Make sure it's user-friendly and visually appealing. But don't stop there localize it! This means translating not just the words but the entire experience. From images to payment options, every detail counts.

Consider this: if you're selling high-end fashion in Italy, you might want to showcase sleek designs and luxury vibes. But if you're targeting budget-conscious shoppers in India, your approach should reflect affordability and practicality.

Now, let's talk social media. Platforms vary in popularity across regions. In the U.S., Facebook and Instagram reign supreme, but in China, you're looking at WeChat and Weibo. Tailor your content for each platform and engage with your audience in a way that feels authentic.

Here's a fun exercise: create a social media content calendar for a month, focusing on a specific country. What local events can you tie your posts to? How can you engage with trends in that market? This will not only boost your visibility but also show that you're invested in their culture.

Data-Driven Decision Making

In the world of global marketing, data is your best friend. It's like having a crystal ball that reveals what your customers want. But here's the catch: you've got to know how to interpret that data effectively.

Start by analyzing customer behavior. What are they buying? When are they buying it? Tools like Google Analytics can provide valuable insights into your audience's preferences. Use this data to refine your strategies and make informed decisions.

Let's say you notice a spike in sales for a particular product in a specific region. Instead of just celebrating the success, dig deeper. What's driving that demand? Is it a seasonal trend, or did a local influencer promote it? Understanding these factors will help you replicate that success in other markets.

And don't forget about A/B testing. This technique allows you to experiment with different marketing strategies and see what resonates best with your audience. Whether it's email subject lines or ad visuals, testing helps you optimize your approach for maximum impact.

Building Relationships through Customer Service

Customer service is often the unsung hero of global marketing. It's not just about solving problems; it's about building relationships. When customers feel valued and understood, they're more likely to become loyal advocates for your brand.

Consider implementing a multi-lingual customer support system. This shows that you're committed to meeting your customers where they are. If a customer in Brazil has a question, they shouldn't have to navigate a language barrier to get help. Providing support in their native language builds trust and fosters a positive experience.

Also, be proactive in seeking feedback. Encourage customers to share their thoughts and experiences. This not only helps you improve your offerings but also makes customers feel heard. It's like asking a friend for their opinion on a new haircut people love to share their thoughts!

And here's a fun challenge: create a customer service training program that emphasizes cultural sensitivity. Equip your team with the skills to handle diverse customer interactions with grace and understanding. This investment will pay off in the long run.

Navigating Legal and Ethical Considerations

As you venture into global markets, it's crucial to navigate the legal and ethical landscape. Each country has its own regulations regarding advertising, data privacy, and consumer rights. Ignoring these can lead to hefty fines or damage to your reputation.

Start by familiarizing yourself with local laws. Consult legal experts who specialize in international business to ensure compliance. This isn't just about avoiding trouble; it's about demonstrating your commitment to ethical practices.

Additionally, be transparent with your customers. If you're collecting data, let them know how it will be used. This builds trust and shows that you respect their privacy. In an age where data breaches make headlines, transparency is key.

Finally, consider your brand's social responsibility. How can you contribute positively to the communities you're engaging with?

Whether it's through sustainable practices or supporting local initiatives, showing that you care goes a long way in building goodwill.

The Road Ahead: Adapting to Change

The global marketplace is ever-evolving, and adaptability is your greatest asset. Trends shift, consumer preferences change, and new technologies emerge. Staying ahead of the curve requires a willingness to embrace change.

Keep an eye on emerging markets. Countries that may not be on your radar today could become the next big thing tomorrow. Invest time in understanding these markets and their potential.

Also, don't be afraid to pivot your strategies. If something isn't working, reassess and adjust. Flexibility is key to thriving in a dynamic environment.

Finally, foster a culture of innovation within your organization. Encourage your team to think outside the box and explore new ideas. The next groundbreaking marketing strategy could come from an unexpected source!

In conclusion, understanding global markets is a multifaceted journey that requires curiosity, respect, and a willingness to learn. It's not just about numbers and stats; it's about connecting with people on a deeper level. By embracing cultural nuances, leveraging digital strategies, and building relationships, you can navigate the complexities of the global marketplace with confidence.

So, what's the next step for you? Dive into research, engage with local communities, and don't shy away from asking questions. The world is your oyster, and with the right approach, you can create a thriving global business that resonates with customers everywhere. Now, let's get out there and make some global waves!

Chapter 2

The Power of E-Commerce

You know what's really mind-blowing? Just how much online shopping has flipped the script on how we buy stuff. I mean, think about it: who doesn't love the idea of kicking back on the couch in their comfiest PJs, munching on popcorn, and browsing for a shiny new pair of shoes all without having to squeeze into real pants? That's the magic of e-commerce, right? It's like this enchanted doorway that whisks you straight into a retail wonderland, all from the comfort of your living room. You can snag everything from quirky cat toys to the latest tech gadgets while binge-watching your favorite series. And let's be honest, sometimes the only workout we get is from clicking that "add to cart" button.

But hey, let's take a moment to really dig into this e-commerce wonderland. Online shopping isn't just a passing fad; it's become a fundamental part of our daily lives. Seriously, the convenience factor is off the charts! Picture this: according to recent stats, over 2.14 billion people worldwide are expected to buy goods and services online in 2021. That's nearly a third of the entire planet! If that doesn't make you sit up and take notice, I don't know what will.

Now, while we're on the topic, let's chat about social media for a sec. It's not just a platform for scrolling through endless pictures of your friend's cat or watching the latest viral dance challenges anymore. Nope! Businesses have wised up to the fact that social media is a goldmine for selling products directly to customers. Just think about it: you're minding your own business, scrolling through Instagram, and BAM! There's an ad for that trendy gadget you didn't even know you needed. Next thing you know, you're hitting that "buy now" button faster than you can say "impulse purchase."

Many businesses are diving into platforms like Facebook, Instagram, and TikTok to whip up engaging content that reels customers in. They're using eye-catching visuals, teaming up with influencers, and running targeted ads to create a shopping experience that feels seamless. It's like shopping at a mall but without the crowds, the harsh lighting, and those questionable food court choices. And guess what? It's working! Social media sales are projected to hit a whopping $600 billion by 2025. That's a serious chunk of change!

But here's the kicker: our trusty mobile phones are shaking things up even more. Remember when you had to plop down at your desktop computer to shop online? Yeah, me neither! Now, we've got shopping apps, mobile websites, and even one-click checkout options that make it ridiculously easy to snag things on the go. Whether you're standing in line at the grocery store or sipping on a latte at your favorite café, you can browse and shop with just a few taps on your phone.

Think about it this way: your mobile phone is like a personal shopping assistant that's always at your side. Need a last-minute gift? Boom! You can order it while waiting for your coffee. Want to compare prices while you're out and about? Easy peasy! The freedom and flexibility that mobile shopping brings are game-changers for both consumers and businesses alike.

So, how can you, as a business owner, tap into this e-commerce revolution? Here are a few practical tips to get you started:

First off, optimize for mobile. Seriously, make sure your website is mobile-friendly. If your site takes forever to load or is a pain to navigate on a phone, you're going to lose potential customers faster than you can say "checkout."

Next up, utilize social media. Create engaging content that showcases your products. Use eye-catching images and videos, and don't shy away from using stories or live videos to connect with your audience. People love that personal touch!

Then there's the importance of implementing seamless payment options. Make it easy for customers to pay. Offering options like Apple Pay, Google Pay, or PayPal can streamline the checkout process and reduce those pesky cart abandonment rates.
Oh, and don't forget to leverage data analytics . Use analytics tools to track customer behavior and preferences. This data can help you tailor your marketing strategies and product offerings to meet the needs of your audience. It's like having a crystal ball for your business!

And here's a big one: engage with your customers. Respond to comments and messages on social media. Building a relationship with your audience can lead to increased brand loyalty and repeat purchases. People want to feel valued, so a little kindness goes a long way.

Now, let's talk about experimenting with influencer marketing. Partner with influencers who align with your brand values. Their endorsement can introduce your products to a whole new audience and boost your credibility. It's like having a trusted friend recommend your stuff!

Now, I know what you might be thinking: "But what if my business is small, or I don't have a huge marketing budget?" Well, here's the deal: you don't need to be a big player to succeed in e-commerce. Start small, focus on building a strong online presence, and gradually scale up as you gain traction. Remember, every big brand started somewhere!

And let's not overlook the importance of customer experience. A smooth, enjoyable shopping experience can turn a one-time buyer into a loyal customer. Make sure your website is easy to navigate, your product descriptions are clear and informative, and your customer service is top-notch. People love to feel valued, and a little kindness goes a long way.

In my own experience, I've seen firsthand how e-commerce can transform a business. A few years back, I started a small online store selling handmade crafts. At first, it was just a side hustle, you know? But I quickly realized the potential of reaching customers beyond my local area. I invested time in learning about social media marketing and mobile optimization, and before I knew it, my little shop was gaining traction. It was exhilarating to see orders rolling in from all over the country!

Now, I'm not saying it was all smooth sailing. There were plenty of late nights, trial and error, and a few hiccups along the way. But the key takeaway here is that e-commerce offers a world of opportunity for those willing to embrace it.

As we move forward in this digital age, it's clear that the power of e-commerce is only going to grow. So, buckle up and get ready to ride the wave! Whether you're a seasoned entrepreneur or just starting out, now is the time to harness the potential of online shopping, social media, and mobile technology. The world is your oyster, and the possibilities are endless!

So, what are you waiting for? Get out there, start exploring the e-commerce landscape, and watch your business thrive! Remember, it's not just about selling products; it's about creating a memorable experience for your customers. And who knows? You might just find yourself in the fast lane of global commerce before you know it. Happy selling!

Now, let's take a moment to reflect on the impact e-commerce has had on our daily lives. Think about those moments when you've been caught in the rain without an umbrella or when you've needed a last-minute birthday gift. E-commerce has swooped in to save the day, allowing us to solve our problems with just a few clicks. It's like having a trusty sidekick that's always there when you need it.

And let's not forget about the thrill of unboxing. You know that feeling when you hear the doorbell ring and your package has finally arrived? Your heart races a little, doesn't it? You rip open the box, and it's like Christmas morning all over again. That's the kind of joy e-commerce can bring not just to you as a shopper but also to your customers. Creating that excitement is part of the magic.

Now, let's talk about the community aspect of e-commerce. It's not just about transactions; it's about connecting with people. You can build a community around your brand, engaging with customers and creating a space where they feel heard and valued. This is where the real power of e-commerce shines. It's not just about selling; it's about building relationships that last.

Think about how you can foster that sense of community. Maybe you start a blog where you share tips and tricks related to your products, or perhaps you host live Q&A sessions on social media. These little touches can help turn casual buyers into loyal fans. They'll come back not just for your products but for the experience you create.

And speaking of experiences, let's dive into the importance of storytelling in e-commerce. People love a good story. It draws them in and makes them feel connected to your brand. Share your journey, the ups and downs, the passion behind what you do. When customers feel a personal connection, they're more likely to support your business. It's like inviting them into your world, and who doesn't want to be part of something special?

You can also tap into user-generated content. Encourage your customers to share their experiences with your products on social media. Maybe they post a photo of themselves using your product or leave a glowing review. This not only provides social proof but also creates a sense of community among your customers. It's like having a whole squad of brand ambassadors cheering you on!

Now, let's not forget about the importance of staying ahead of the curve. E-commerce is always evolving, and it's crucial to keep up with the latest trends and technologies. Whether it's exploring augmented reality for virtual try-ons or using Chatbots for customer service, staying innovative can set you apart from the competition. Embrace change, and don't be afraid to experiment with new ideas.

And while we're at it, let's talk about sustainability. More and more consumers are looking for eco-friendly options. If you can incorporate sustainable practices into your business model, you'll not only attract environmentally conscious customers but also contribute to a better world. It's a win-win!

As we wrap up this journey through the power of e-commerce, remember that it's not just about selling products; it's about creating experiences, building relationships, and making a positive impact. The digital landscape is filled with opportunities waiting for you to seize them. So, take that leap of faith, dive into the world of e-commerce, and watch your business flourish.

In the end, it's all about connecting with people, sharing your passion, and making their lives a little brighter. So, go ahead, embrace the power of e-commerce, and let your dreams take flight. The world is waiting for you, and I can't wait to see what you create! Happy selling, my friend!

Chapter 3

Millions of potential buyers

When you think about social media, what pops into your head? Is it those adorable cat videos? Or maybe it's the endless stream of memes that seem to be everywhere? Well, buckle up, because there's a whole other side to social media that's a total game-changer for businesses. I'm here to let you in on how to harness its power to reach a global audience. Just imagine this for a second: you've got an amazing product, and with just a few clicks, you can connect with MILLIONS of potential buyers. Sounds like a fairy tale, right? But trust me, it's not just wishful thinking it's the reality we're living in today.

So, let's break it down a bit. Social media platforms like Facebook, Instagram, and TikTok are way more than just places to share selfies or your latest meal. They've turned into bustling marketplaces where brands can show off their products and actually engage with customers. It's like having a storefront on the busiest street in the world and the best part? You don't even have to pay rent! You can reach people all over the globe without ever leaving your couch. Pretty wild, huh?

Now, you might be sitting there thinking, "Okay, but how do I even get started?" Here's the scoop: first, you need to pick the right platform for your audience. Are you selling trendy clothes? Instagram is definitely your go-to. If you're in the B2B game, LinkedIn might be more your style. A little research goes a long way, and don't be afraid to experiment a bit. The beauty of social media is that you can dip your toes in without having to dive in headfirst.

Once you've set up your little shop on your chosen platform, it's time to get social like, really social. Engage with your audience! Respond to comments, share behind-the-scenes content, and don't shy away from asking for feedback. Think of it like throwing a party and inviting everyone to join in on the fun. People love feeling like they're part of something bigger, and when they see that you genuinely care about what they have to say, they're way more likely to stick around. Plus, building that trust can turn casual followers into die-hard fans.

Speaking of fans, let's chat about influencers for a second. These folks have really nailed the art of persuasion. They can take your product and make it look like the hottest trend since, well, sliced bread. Imagine them as the cool kids in high school who can get everyone to rock the same brand of sneakers. Partnering with influencers can seriously boost your visibility and sales. But here's a little pro tip: make sure you choose influencers whose values line up with your brand. If you're all about eco-friendly products, teaming up with someone who promotes sustainability makes way more sense than partnering with someone who's all about fast fashion.

But hey, don't just take my word for it. Look at the numbers! A recent study found that 49% of consumers rely on influencer recommendations when making purchase decisions. That's almost half! So, if you're not tapping into this goldmine, you're missing out on a huge opportunity.

Now, let's circle back to engaging with your customers. You know what they say: "A happy customer is a repeat customer." When you interact with your audience on social media, you're not just pushing products; you're building real relationships. Share user-generated content, run contests, and ask for their opinions. It's like having a heart-to-heart over coffee except this coffee is brewed in a virtual café where everyone's invited.

And here's a little secret: people love sharing their experiences. When they post about your product, it's basically free advertising! Encourage them to tag you in their posts or use a specific hashtag. You'll start to create a community around your brand, and that sense of belonging can be incredibly powerful.

Alright, let's talk about some practical steps to get this ball rolling. Here's a quick checklist to help you harness the power of social media:

1. Identify your target audience. Seriously, know who you're talking to!
2. Choose the right platform(s) for your brand.
3. Create a content calendar to plan out your posts. Trust me, it'll save you a ton of headaches later.
4. Engage with your followers regularly. Don't just post and ghost!
5. Collaborate with influencers who genuinely align with your brand's mission.
6. Keep an eye on your analytics to see what's working and what's not.

Remember, Rome wasn't built in a day, and neither is a solid social media presence. It takes time and consistency. But hey, don't get discouraged! Celebrate the small wins along the way. Did a post go viral? High-five! Did you gain a few new followers? Awesome! Every little step counts.

As you dive into the world of social media, keep this in mind: it's not just about selling products; it's about creating connections. When you treat your audience like friends rather than just customers, you'll see some real magic happen. They'll become your brand advocates, spreading the word and bringing in new buyers faster than you can say "viral marketing."

So, let's get a little deeper into the nitty-gritty of how to make your social media presence not just effective, but downright engaging. First off, let's talk about content. You want to create posts that resonate with your audience. Think about what they care about, what makes them tick, and how your product fits into their lives. It's not just about showcasing your product; it's about telling a story.

For instance, if you're selling handmade candles, don't just post a picture of the candle. Share a story about how you started making them, the inspiration behind your scents, or even how they can enhance a cozy night in. Use sensory language describe the warmth of the flickering flame, the calming scent of lavender, and how it transforms a space into a sanctuary. You want your audience to feel something, to connect with your brand on a deeper level.

Visuals are also super important. A well-crafted image or video can grab attention faster than a catchy caption. Use high-quality photos, and don't be afraid to get creative with your visuals. Show your product in action, or even better, let your customers do the talking by featuring their photos using your product. It adds authenticity and helps build that community vibe we talked about earlier.

Now, let's not forget about the power of storytelling. People love a good story. Share behind-the-scenes glimpses of your business journey, the challenges you've faced, and the triumphs you've celebrated. It makes your brand relatable and human. You're not just a faceless company; you're a person with a passion, and that's something people can connect with.

And speaking of connection, let's chat about the importance of responding to your audience. If someone takes the time to comment on your post or send you a message, acknowledge them!

It's like having a conversation in real life you wouldn't just ignore someone who spoke to you, right? Engaging with your audience shows that you value their input and care about their experience. Plus, it encourages others to join in on the conversation.

Now, let's dive into the world of hashtags. You might be thinking, "Do I really need to bother with hashtags?" The answer is yes! Hashtags are like little signposts that help people find your content. But don't just throw a bunch of random hashtags together. Do a bit of research and find out which ones are relevant to your niche. You want to use a mix of popular hashtags and some that are more niche-specific. This way, you'll increase your chances of being discovered by the right audience.

And while we're on the topic of discovery, let's talk about the power of user-generated content. When your customers share their experiences with your product, it's pure gold. Encourage them to tag you in their posts or use a specific hashtag you've created. Not only does this provide you with free content to share, but it also builds a sense of community around your brand. Plus, it shows potential customers that real people love your product, which can be incredibly persuasive.

Now, let's shift gears a bit and talk about consistency. This is key in the world of social media. You don't want to post once and then disappear for weeks. Create a content calendar to plan out your posts and keep your audience engaged. Consistency helps build trust, and when your audience knows they can count on you for regular content, they're more likely to stick around.

And don't forget to analyze your performance! Social media platforms offer a treasure trove of analytics that can help you understand what's working and what's not. Are certain types of posts getting more engagement? Is there a particular time when your audience is most active? Use this information to refine your strategy and make informed decisions moving forward.

Now, let's wrap things up with a little reminder. Social media is a tool, and like any tool, it's all about how you use it. It's not just about pushing products; it's about building relationships and creating a community. So, grab that digital hammer and start building your brand's online presence. Who knows? You might just find yourself with a billion buyers at your fingertips. Now, that's what I call a win-win!

So, as you embark on this social media journey, keep your heart in it. Be genuine, be relatable, and don't be afraid to show your personality. Your audience wants to connect with a real person, not just a brand. When you create that connection, you'll see your social media presence flourish, and who knows? You might just change the game for your business in ways you never imagined. Now, go out there and make some waves!

Chapter 4

Understanding local customs

Let's chat about something super important when it comes to taking your business global: adapting to local cultures. Now, I can already hear some of you thinking, "Why should I bother with local customs? I've got an amazing product!" But, hold on just a minute! Just because you've got the next big thing doesn't mean it'll fly off the shelves everywhere you go.

Imagine this: you're an ambitious entrepreneur, ready to launch your brand-new line of hot sauce. You're thinking, "Everyone loves spicy food, right?" But here's the kicker in some cultures, spicy isn't just a flavor; it's practically a way of life. If you don't get that, you might as well be tossing your hot sauce into a volcano. Seriously, talk about a recipe for disaster!

Understanding local customs is like having a secret map that leads straight to the treasure chest of customer loyalty. When you take the time to learn about the people and their ways, you can sidestep some major pitfalls that could seriously offend potential buyers. It's all about respect, folks.

Let's break it down a bit. Here are some local customs you should keep in mind:

First up, greetings. In some places, a firm handshake is a sign of confidence and strength. But in others, it's all about a gentle touch or even a bow. You really need to know your audience here! A misstep in greetings can set the wrong tone right from the start.

Next, we've got dining etiquette. If you're lucky enough to get invited to a meal, don't just waltz in with your American table manners. Oh no, my friend! You need to learn the local dining customs like when it's appropriate to eat, what you should bring, and how to behave at the table. Trust me, showing up with the wrong expectations can be a real faux pas.

And let's not forget about dress codes. Some cultures are all about casual wear, while others expect you to show up in a suit and tie. You want to dress to impress, but don't go overboard. Finding that sweet spot can make all the difference in how you're perceived.

Now, let's dive into something that might surprise you: local holidays. You might be thinking, "Holidays? What do they have to do with my business?" Well, let me tell you, they're like hidden gold! Picture this: you launch a marketing campaign that ties into a local festival. It's like hitting the jackpot!

Here's how you can make the most of local holidays:

First off, create special promotions. Offer discounts or themed products that resonate with the holiday spirit. If it's Halloween, for instance, why not whip up a spooky-themed version of your product? People love a good seasonal tie-in, and it can really boost your sales.

Next, engage with the community. Sponsor local events or participate in parades. This isn't just good PR; it's a way to connect with your customers on a personal level. When people see you actively involved in their community, they're more likely to support your business.

And don't forget to share local stories! Use your platform to highlight local traditions and customs. It shows you genuinely care about the community, and that can go a long way in building trust. People want to do business with those who understand and appreciate their culture.

Now, let's chat about localizing your products. This isn't just about slapping a new label on something and calling it a day; it's about making your product truly resonate with your target market. Think about it: if you're selling snacks, wouldn't you want to offer flavors that locals love? It's all about giving people what they want.

Here are some tips for product localization:

First, research local tastes. What flavors are popular? What ingredients do people love? You might be surprised at what people in other countries crave. For example, in some Asian countries, sweet and savory flavors are a hit, while in others, they might prefer something spicier.

Next, design matters. Colors and designs can have different meanings in different cultures. You definitely want to make sure your product packaging doesn't accidentally offend or confuse anyone. It's worth taking the time to get this right.

And here's a big one: test, test, and test! Before launching a localized product, do some focus groups. Get feedback from locals. You want to hit the ground running, not face plant into a wall. Trust me, a little bit of research can save you a lot of headaches down the line.

Alright, let's wrap this up with some actionable steps you can take right now:

First, do your homework. Research the cultures you're entering. Understand their customs, holidays, and preferences. The more you know, the better equipped you'll be to connect with your audience.

Next, engage locally. Reach out to local influencers or community leaders. They can provide insights and help you navigate the waters. Having a local ally can make a world of difference.

And don't be afraid to be flexible. If something isn't working, change it up! Listen to feedback and adjust your strategy accordingly. The ability to pivot can be a game-changer in the business world.

Finally, celebrate your successes! When your localized product flies off the shelves, take a moment to celebrate. Share those wins with your team and your community. It's a great way to build morale and keep everyone motivated.

In conclusion, adapting to local cultures isn't just a nice-to-have; it's a must-have. It's about building bridges, not walls. When you take the time to understand and respect local customs, celebrate local holidays, and localize your products, you're not just selling; you're creating a connection. And that connection? That's what keeps customers coming back for more.

So, are you ready to take your global business to the next level? Let's roll up our sleeves and get to work!

Now, let's dig a little deeper into why all this matters. Picture this: you're in a new country, and you're trying to sell your product. You think you've got everything figured out, but then you realize you've overlooked something crucial. Maybe it's a cultural norm that you didn't know about, or perhaps it's a local preference that you didn't take into account. Suddenly, your amazing product isn't so amazing in the eyes of your potential customers.

It's a bit like throwing a party and forgetting to send out invitations. You might have the best snacks and music, but if no one knows about it, you're going to be sitting there alone, eating chips and wondering where everyone is.

And let's be real here: no one wants to be that person. You want to be the life of the party, the one everyone wants to hang out with. To do that, you've got to understand the vibe of the crowd. You've got to know what makes them tick, what gets them excited, and what might turn them off.

Think about it this way: when you travel to a new place, don't you love it when the locals share their favorite spots with you? It feels special, right? You're getting an insider's view, and it makes your experience that much richer. That's exactly what you want to create with your business. You want to be the brand that feels local, that understands the heartbeat of the community.

And let's not forget about the emotional side of things. When you respect and celebrate local cultures, you're not just building a customer base; you're building relationships. You're showing people that you care about them and their way of life. That kind of connection can turn a one-time buyer into a lifelong customer.

So, what's the takeaway here? It's simple: adapt, learn, and grow. The world is a big place, and there's so much to discover. Embrace the differences, celebrate the uniqueness of each culture, and let that guide your business decisions.

And remember, it's not just about making a sale. It's about making a difference. When you take the time to understand and adapt to local cultures, you're not just expanding your business; you're enriching your own life and the lives of those around you.

So, let's get out there and make some waves in the global market. It's time to connect, adapt, and thrive!

Chapter 5

Sustainable Practices

Let's talk about something that's not just a buzzword anymore sustainability. Now, I know what you're thinking: "Oh great, another lecture on saving the planet." But hear me out! This isn't just about hugging trees and saving the whales. It's about making smart business moves that can seriously boost your bottom line. Yep, you heard me right. Many consumers today prefer to buy from companies that are environmentally friendly. So, if you're not on this train yet, you might want to hop on before it leaves the station!

Think about it: when was the last time you made a purchase based on a brand's commitment to the environment? If you're anything like me, it probably wasn't too long ago. It's like choosing between a burger from a fast-food joint and a locally sourced, grass-fed beef burger. One feels good for your taste buds, but the other feels good for your conscience. It's a no-brainer, right? This preference for sustainable practices isn't just a trend; it's a fundamental shift in consumer behavior. If you're not tapping into this, you're missing out on a goldmine of potential buyers.

Using sustainable materials can be a game-changer. Imagine you're running a clothing line. You could use conventional materials, or you could source organic cotton, recycled polyester, or even innovative fabrics made from pineapple leaves (yes, that's a thing!). Not only does this attract customers who care about the planet, but it also gives your brand a unique selling point. It's like having a secret weapon in your back pocket! When customers see that you're committed to sustainability, they're more likely to choose you over competitors who aren't.

And let's not forget about the brand image. Businesses that practice sustainability can improve their reputation in a big way. Think of it this way: if you're known for being environmentally conscious, you're not just selling products; you're selling values. This can lead to a loyal customer base that feels good about supporting your brand. Plus, word of mouth is a powerful tool. Happy customers will rave about you to their friends, and before you know it, you've built a community around your brand.

But wait, let's break this down a bit more. Here are some practical tips to get you started on your sustainable journey:

1. Audit Your Supply Chain: Take a hard look at where your materials come from. Are they sustainably sourced? If not, it's time to make some changes.

2. Communicate Your Efforts: Don't be shy! Let your customers know what you're doing to be more sustainable. Use social media, your website, and even product packaging to share your story.

3. Get certified: Look into certifications like Fair Trade or organic labels. These can give your brand a credibility boost and attract more eco-conscious consumers.

4. Engage with Your Community: Participate in local environmental initiatives or partner with organizations that promote sustainability. It's a win-win; you're helping the planet and enhancing your brand image.

5. Be Transparent: Consumers appreciate honesty. If you're working towards sustainability but haven't hit the mark yet, share your goals and progress. People love a good underdog story!

Now, you might be wondering, "But what if my competitors are doing the same thing?" Great question! Here's the kicker: while many businesses are jumping on the sustainability bandwagon, not all of them are doing it authentically. If you can show genuine commitment and passion for sustainable practices, you'll stand out in a crowded market. Think of it like being the only kid in school who actually does their homework. Sure, some might try to cheat off you, but they can't replicate your hard work and dedication.

Let's talk numbers for a second. A Nielsen report found that 66% of consumers are willing to pay more for sustainable brands. That's a significant chunk of change! If you're not considering sustainability in your business model, you're potentially leaving money on the table. And let's be real; who wants to do that?

But it's not just about the dollars and cents. It's about creating a legacy. By adopting sustainable practices, you're contributing to a better world for future generations. You're not just a business owner; you're a steward of the planet. How cool is that?

Now, let's address some misconceptions. Some folks might think that going green is too expensive or complicated. Sure, there might be an initial investment, but think of it as planting a seed. It might take some time to grow, but once it does, the fruits of your labor will be worth it. Plus, many sustainable practices can actually save you money in the long run. For example, using energy-efficient equipment can lower your utility bills. It's like getting a discount on your overhead costs who wouldn't want that?

And let's not overlook the tech side of things. There are tons of tools and resources out there to help you on your sustainable journey. From apps that track your carbon footprint to platforms that connect you with eco-friendly suppliers, the digital age has made it easier than ever to go green. Embrace it!

So, what's the takeaway here? Embracing sustainable practices isn't just good for the planet; it's good for business. It can improve your brand image, attract new customers, and even save you money in the long run. Plus, you get to feel good about the impact you're making. It's a win-win!

Now, here's a little challenge for you: take a moment to reflect on your business practices. What's one small change you can make today to move towards sustainability? Maybe it's switching to biodegradable packaging or sourcing materials from local suppliers. Whatever it is, take that first step. You'll be surprised at how quickly it can snowball into something bigger.

Remember, every little bit counts. Just like those tiny drops of water that can eventually fill a bucket, your efforts can lead to significant change. So, roll up your sleeves and get to work! The world and your customers will thank you for it.

Chapter 6

The Importance of Customer Feedback

Let's chat about something that's often overlooked but oh-so-crucial: CUSTOMER FEEDBACK. Seriously, if you want your business to thrive, you've got to pay attention to what your customers are saying. Think of it like tuning into a radio station if you're not listening to the right frequency, you're going to miss out on some great tunes.

First off, let's talk about the importance of LISTENING. You know that saying, "You've got two ears and one mouth for a reason"? Well, it's true! Listening to what customers say can help businesses improve their products and services. Picture this: you're at a restaurant, and the waiter asks how your meal is. You tell him it's too salty. If he takes that feedback to the chef, guess what? The chef can adjust the recipe for next time. It's a win-win!

Now, you might be wondering, "How do I even get this feedback?" That's where surveys and reviews come into play. These tools are like gold mines for businesses. They provide valuable insights into what customers really want. It's not just about asking if they liked the product; it's about digging deeper. You want to know what they loved, what they hated, and what they wish they could change.

Here's a quick tip: Keep your surveys short and sweet. Nobody wants to fill out a novel-length questionnaire. Aim for 5-10 questions that get straight to the point. Use multiple-choice questions for quick answers, but don't shy away from open-ended questions that let customers spill their guts. You might be surprised at the gems you uncover.

And let's not forget about the power of online reviews. They're like the modern-day word-of-mouth, and they can make or break your business. Did you know that 93% of consumers read online reviews before making a purchase? That's right! So, if you're not paying attention to what's being said about your brand, you're missing out on a huge opportunity to learn and grow.

Now, let's talk about complaints. I know, I know nobody likes to hear negative feedback. But here's the thing: addressing customer complaints quickly can turn unhappy buyers into loyal ones. It's like a superhero move! You swoop in, resolve their issue, and suddenly they're singing your praises.

Think about it: if a customer reaches out with a problem, they're giving you a chance to shine. Respond promptly and empathetically. A simple, "Hey, I'm really sorry to hear that you had a bad experience. Let's make it right," can go a long way. And if you can offer a solution like a refund, replacement, or discount you'll not only fix the issue but also show that you value their business.

Here's a little story for you. A few months back, I ordered a pair of shoes online. When they arrived, they were the wrong size. I shot off an email to customer service, half-expecting a long wait or a "too bad, so sad" response. Instead, I got a reply within an hour! They apologized, sent me the correct size, and even threw in a discount for my next purchase. You better believe I'll be a loyal customer now.

So, how can you make the most of customer feedback? Here's a quick list of actionable steps:

1. Create a Feedback Loop: Set up regular intervals for gathering feedback. This could be after a purchase, a service interaction, or even a few weeks later.

2. Use Multiple Channels: Don't just rely on one method. Use surveys, social media, email, and face-to-face interactions to gather insights.

3. Analyze the Data: Take a good look at the feedback you receive. Look for trends and common themes. What are customers raving about? What are they complaining about?

4. Implement Changes: Don't just collect feedback for the sake of it. Use it to make real changes in your business.

5. Follow Up: After making changes, reach out to customers to let them know. "Thanks for your feedback! We've made some changes based on what you told us." This shows you care and keeps the lines of communication open.

6. Celebrate Successes: When you receive positive feedback, share it! Highlight customer testimonials on your website or social media. It builds credibility and encourages others to share their experiences.

Now, let's talk about the tech side of things. There are plenty of tools out there that can help you gather and analyze customer feedback. Platforms like Survey Monkey or Google Forms make it easy to create surveys, while tools like Trust pilot or Yelp can help you manage reviews. Find what works for you and your business.

In conclusion, customer feedback isn't just a nice-to-have; it's a MUST-HAVE. It's your secret weapon for improving products, enhancing customer service, and building loyalty. So, get out there and start listening! Your customers are ready to share their thoughts, and you've got a golden opportunity to turn that feedback into action. Remember, it's all about creating a better experience for your customers, and in turn, they'll create a better future for your business.

So, what are you waiting for? Dive into those surveys, respond to those reviews, and watch your business flourish!

Chapter 7

Building a Strong Brand: Your Path to Standing Out

Alright, let's dive into something that's super important if you're running a business today building a strong brand. Seriously, in this crazy, crowded marketplace, it's like trying to find a needle in a haystack. There are a million brands out there all scrambling for attention, and let's face it, a lot of them look pretty much the same. So, how do you make your business pop? How do you make it not just another face in the crowd? The answer lies in crafting a STRONG BRAND.

Now, I'm not talking about just slapping a logo on a product and calling it a day. Nope, my friend, it's way deeper than that. It's about creating a memorable identity that sticks in your customers' minds like that catchy tune you can't shake off. You know the one I'm talking about the one that gets stuck in your head when you least expect it.

Think about it for a second. When you hear the name "Nike," what comes to mind? I bet it's that iconic swoosh and the phrase "Just Do

It." That's branding at its best, folks! A recognizable brand can make your business stand out like a unicorn in a field of horses. It's your ticket not just to being noticed but also to being remembered. And in this digital age, let me tell you, that's worth its weight in gold.

So, how do you get to that point? First things first, CONSISTENCY is your best friend. You want your messaging and visuals to be as cohesive as a well-rehearsed band. Your logo, color scheme, and tone of voice should all align like a perfectly tuned guitar. If your brand is all over the place, trust me, your customers will be too. They won't know what to expect, and you really want them to know exactly what they're getting when they see your brand.

Let's break this down with a quick checklist to help ensure your brand stays consistent:

1. Define your brand's mission and values. Seriously, what do you stand for? What gets you out of bed in the morning?
2. Create a style guide. This should outline your logo usage, color palette, and typography. Think of it as your brand's playbook.
3. Make sure your messaging aligns with your brand's personality. Are you fun and quirky, or serious and professional?

4. Regularly review your marketing materials to ensure they reflect your brand accurately. It's like giving your brand a little check-up now and then.

Now, let's chat about the magic of loyal customers. A strong brand doesn't just attract buyers; it creates FANS. You know, the kind of people who'll rave about your product to their friends, family, and even their pets! These loyal customers become your brand ambassadors, and they can do wonders for your business. Word-of-mouth? It's still one of the most powerful marketing tools out there, no question about it.

But how do you cultivate that loyalty? It all boils down to delivering VALUE. When customers feel like they're getting something special from your brand whether it's top-notch customer service, high-quality products, or even a sense of community they're way more likely to stick around.

Here are some strategies to help foster that loyalty:
- Engage with your customers on social media. Respond to their comments and messages like you're chatting with a friend. Trust me, it makes a world of difference.

- Offer exclusive deals or early access to new products for repeat customers. Who doesn't love a good deal, right?
- Create a loyalty program that rewards customers for their purchases. It's like a frequent flyer program but for shopping!
- Share customer testimonials and success stories. Let your fans do the talking for you!

Now, I know what you might be thinking: "But how do I know if my branding is working?" That's a fantastic question! You can track your brand's effectiveness through various metrics. Look at customer retention rates, social media engagement, and even sales figures. If you're seeing growth in these areas, chances are you're on the right track.

Let's not forget about the importance of visual identity. A strong brand is like a well-crafted movie poster it draws people in and tells them what to expect. Your visuals should communicate your brand's essence without saying a word. Think about your favorite brands. What do their logos look like? What colors do they use?

Here's a fun little exercise for you: Take a look at your competitors' branding. What do you like or dislike about their visual identity?

Use that insight to refine your own. You want your brand to be distinct, but you also want it to resonate with your target audience. It's a balancing act, but when you nail it, the results can be downright magical.

And let's not overlook the emotional connection. People don't just buy products; they buy feelings. They want to feel good about their purchases, and a strong brand can evoke those feelings. Think of Apple. They don't just sell tech gadgets; they sell a lifestyle. They make you feel like you're part of something bigger than yourself.

So, how can you create that emotional connection? Here are some tips:

- Share your brand story. People love to know the "why" behind a brand. What inspired you to start your business? What's your journey been like?
- Use storytelling in your marketing. Create relatable narratives that resonate with your audience. It's all about making that personal connection.
- Highlight your brand's impact. Are you giving back to the community or using sustainable practices? Don't be shy about sharing that!

Building a strong brand isn't just a one-and-done deal. Nope, it's an ongoing process that requires attention and care. You've got to keep your finger on the pulse of your audience and be willing to adapt as trends change. Remember, even the best brands evolve over time.

So, let's recap what we've covered so far:

- A recognizable brand helps you stand out in a crowded market.
- Consistency in messaging and visuals is crucial for brand recall.
- Strong brands foster customer loyalty, leading to recommendations and repeat business.

Now, I challenge you to take action. Spend some time defining your brand's mission and values. Create that style guide if you haven't already. And don't be afraid to get creative with your visuals. After all, your brand is your baby, and it deserves the best!

Building a strong brand is like planting a tree. It takes time, effort, and a little bit of nurturing, but the fruits of your labor will be worth it. You'll create a legacy that resonates with your customers and stands the test of time. So, roll up your sleeves and get to work. Your brand's bright future is waiting!

Let's dig a little deeper into some of these points, shall we?

When we talk about defining your brand's mission and values, think of it as the foundation of your brand's house. It's what holds everything up and keeps it sturdy. You need to ask yourself some tough questions: What do you believe in? What drives you? Your mission statement should be clear and concise, something that can be easily communicated to your team and your customers. This isn't just for show; it's the guiding star for all your branding efforts.

Now, about that style guide this is like your brand's playbook. It's where you lay down the law on how your brand should look and feel. Your logo should be prominently featured, and you should outline how it should be used. Is it okay to stretch it? Can it be placed on a busy background? What about color variations? These are all important details. Your color palette should evoke the feelings you want your customers to associate with your brand. Colors can evoke emotions like blue for trust or red for excitement.

And typography? Don't underestimate it! The font you choose can say a lot about your brand. A playful font might work for a children's brand, but a sleek, modern font might be better for a tech company.

Next up, let's talk about messaging. Your tone of voice is like the personality of your brand. Are you friendly and approachable, or more formal and authoritative? This tone should be consistent across all your platforms whether it's your website, social media, or even email newsletters. If your brand were a person, how would they speak? Would they crack jokes, or would they keep it professional?

Now, let's dive a bit deeper into customer loyalty. This is where the magic happens. It's one thing to get a sale, but it's another thing entirely to turn that customer into a loyal fan. Think about it: when was the last time you bought something from a brand you love? You probably felt a little thrill, right? That's the kind of feeling you want to create for your customers.

One way to do this is by creating a community around your brand. Social media is a fantastic platform for this. You can engage with your customers, share behind-the-scenes looks at your business, and even highlight customer stories. People love feeling like they're part of something.

And let's not forget about those exclusive deals. Everyone loves a good bargain, right? Offering your loyal customers early access to sales or special promotions can make them feel valued. It's like giving them a VIP pass to your brand.

Now, let's circle back to those metrics I mentioned earlier. You can't manage what you don't measure, right? Keep an eye on your customer retention rates. If you notice that people are coming back for more; that's a great sign that, your branding is resonating. Social media engagement is another key metric. Are people liking, sharing, and commenting on your posts? That's engagement, and it shows that your brand is connecting with your audience.

And of course, sales figures are important. If you're seeing growth, that's fantastic! But don't just look at the numbers in isolation. Try to understand the story behind them. What campaigns worked? What didn't? This analysis will help you refine your approach moving forward.

Let's not forget about the visuals. I mean, who doesn't love a good logo? Your logo is often the first thing people see, so it needs to make an impression. It should be simple yet memorable. Think about some of the most iconic logos out there McDonald's golden arches, the Starbucks mermaid, or swoosh of Nike. These logos are instantly recognizable, and that's what you want for your brand.

And here's a little pro tip: make sure your visuals are adaptable. They should look great on everything from your website to your social media pages to your packaging. Consistency is key, but flexibility is important too.

Now, let's chat about that emotional connection again. This is where storytelling comes into play. People love stories. They connect with them. So, when you share your brand story, make it personal. Talk about the challenges you faced, the triumphs you celebrated, and the lessons you learned along the way.

This doesn't just humanize your brand; it makes it relatable. Your audience will see themselves in your story, and that's powerful. They'll feel a connection to your brand that goes beyond just the products you sell.

And don't forget to highlight your brand's impact. If you're involved in community service or using sustainable practices, shout it from the rooftops! People love supporting brands that give back or are environmentally conscious. It makes them feel good about their purchases, and it builds trust.

As we wrap this up, I want to emphasize that building a strong brand is an ongoing journey. It's not something you can just set and forget. You need to stay engaged with your audience, keep an eye on trends, and be willing to adapt.

Remember, even the best brands have to evolve. So, keep your brand fresh and relevant. Listen to your customers, learn from your mistakes, and celebrate your wins.

So, here's your call to action: take some time to really think about your brand. Define your mission and values, create that style guide, and start building those emotional connections. Your brand is more than just a logo; it's a living, breathing entity that deserves your attention and care.

Building a strong brand is like planting a tree. It takes time, effort, and a little bit of nurturing, but the fruits of your labor will be worth it. You'll create a legacy that resonates with your customers and stands the test of time. So, roll up your sleeves and get to work. Your brand's bright future is waiting, and I can't wait to see what you create!

Chapter 8

Effective Marketing Strategies

Let's dive into the heart of what makes businesses tick marketing. It's the lifeblood of any venture, whether you're a local bakery or a global tech giant. So, how do you reach the right people? How do you get your message across without shouting into the void? Well, grab a seat, because we're about to unpack some solid strategies that'll help you connect with your audience like a warm hug on a chilly day.

First things first, let's talk about the variety of marketing techniques out there. There's no one-size-fits-all approach here. Think of marketing like a buffet there are different dishes to choose from, and you gotta find what suits your taste buds. Email campaigns, social media ads, content marketing you name it, they all serve a purpose. Here's the kicker: each technique reaches different audiences.

1. Email Campaigns: These bad boys are like the classic letter from a friend. They can be personal, engaging, and downright effective if

done right. You can segment your audience and send tailored messages that resonate with them. Imagine receiving an email that feels like it was crafted just for you. Pretty sweet, huh?

2. Online Ads: These are your flashy neon signs. They grab attention and can be targeted to specific demographics. Want to reach young tech enthusiasts? There's a platform for that. Looking to catch the eye of busy moms? You bet there's a way to do that too.

3. Social Media: This is where the magic happens. It's like a giant playground where you can interact with your audience in real-time. Post a funny meme, share a behind-the-scenes look at your business, or run a contest. The possibilities are endless! Just remember to keep it authentic people can smell a phony from a mile away.

Now, let's get to the juicy part: understanding your target demographics. This is crucial. If you don't know who you're talking to, how can you expect to have a conversation? It's like trying to sell ice to Eskimos. You need to know their age, interests, location, and buying habits. Use surveys, social media insights, and good old-fashioned research to gather this data.

Why is this so important? Because when you understand your audience, you can create advertisements that hit home. Here's a little secret: effective ads speak directly to the heart of the viewer. They evoke emotions, tell stories, and offer solutions. Think about it when was the last time you saw an ad that made you go, "Wow, they really get me"?

Next up, let's get creative. Creative marketing is like a magician pulling a rabbit out of a hat. It captures attention and makes your products more desirable. Remember the last time you saw an ad that made you chuckle or think, "That's clever"? That's the kind of creativity we're talking about!

Here are a few ideas to get those creative juices flowing:

- Use storytelling: People love stories. They connect with them. Share your brand's journey, your customers' success stories, or even a day in the life of your product. It makes your brand relatable.

- Visuals matter: We live in a visual world. Use eye-catching images, infographics, and videos to convey your message. A picture is worth a thousand words, right? So, make those visuals count!

- Engage your audience: Ask questions, run polls, or encourage user-generated content. When people feel involved, they're more likely to connect with your brand.

- Be bold: Don't be afraid to take risks. A quirky campaign can set you apart from the competition. Just remember to stay true to your brand voice.

Now, let's get real for a moment. Marketing isn't just about throwing spaghetti at the wall and seeing what sticks. It's about strategy and analysis. You need to measure your efforts and adjust accordingly. Use tools like Google Analytics to track your campaign performance. What's working? What's not?

Let's not forget the power of A/B testing. This is where you can experiment with different versions of your ads to see which one resonates more with your audience. It's like being a mad scientist in the lab tweaking, testing, and discovering what works best.

And speaking of testing, have you ever thought about how to make your marketing more personalized? Tailoring your approach can be a game-changer. Imagine receiving an email that knows your name, your preferences, and even suggests products based on your previous purchases. Feels special, doesn't it?

Personalization can be achieved through data analysis. Use customer data responsibly to create targeted campaigns. Remember, it's not about bombarding your audience with ads; it's about providing them with value.

In this digital age, the landscape is constantly changing. Stay updated on industry trends and be ready to pivot your strategies. What worked last year might not work today. Keep your finger on the pulse of your market and adapt accordingly.

Before we wrap up, let's recap the key takeaways:

- Use a variety of marketing techniques to reach different audiences.
- Understand your target demographics to create effective advertisements.
- Get creative! Use storytelling, visuals, and bold ideas to capture attention.
- Measure your efforts and adjust your strategies based on performance.

- Personalize your marketing approach to make customers feel valued.

Now, it's your turn. Take a moment to reflect on your current marketing strategies. What's working? What could use a little sprucing up? Don't be afraid to experiment and think outside the box. The world of marketing is your oyster, and with the right strategies, you can reach that billion buyers you've been dreaming about.

So, roll up your sleeves, get creative, and let's make some marketing magic happen!

Chapter 9

Logistics and Supply Chain

Efficient delivery systems are the backbone of any successful business, especially when you're trying to reach a global market. Think about it: when you order something online, what do you want? You want it FAST. You want it in one piece. And you want to be able to track it every step of the way. If any of those pieces are missing, you're left feeling like a kid on Christmas morning who just found out Santa forgot to stop by. Not cool, right?

So, how do you keep customers happy? By mastering your logistics and supply chain! It's not just about getting products from point A to point B; it's about creating a seamless experience that keeps customers coming back for more. Here's the kicker: if your delivery system is slow or unreliable, you can bet your bottom dollar that customers will take their business elsewhere.

Now, let's talk about global shipping options. If you're aiming for a worldwide audience, you've got to understand the ins and outs of shipping. It's like navigating a maze with a million twists and turns.

You've got air freight, sea freight, express services, and all sorts of options in between. Each method has its pros and cons, and choosing the right one can make or break your business.

Here's a quick rundown of global shipping options:

1. Air Freight: Fast but often pricey. Perfect for urgent deliveries.
2. Sea Freight: Cost-effective for large shipments but can take weeks. Ideal for bulk goods.
3. Express Services: Think FedEx or DHL. Quick and reliable, but costs can add up.
4. Local Couriers: Great for last-mile delivery. They know the area like the back of their hand.

Understanding these options can help you reach more customers faster. You can even offer different shipping methods at checkout, giving customers the power to choose what works best for them. It's like letting them pick their own adventure!

Now, let's shift gears to inventory management. Picture this: you've got a hot new product that everyone wants, but you're out of stock. Ouch! That's a missed opportunity and a surefire way to frustrate your customers. Good inventory management ensures that products are available when customers want them. It's all about keeping the right amount of stock on hand. Too much inventory? You're tying up cash and risking spoilage. Too little? You're losing sales.

Here are some tips to keep your inventory in check:

- Use Inventory Management Software: Tools like Trade Gecko or Fishbowl can help you track stock levels in real-time.
- Set Reorder Points: Know when to restock before you run out. It's like knowing when to refill your coffee before it runs dry.
- Analyze Sales Trends: Look at past sales data to predict future demand. It's like reading the tea leaves, but way more reliable.
- Conduct Regular Audits: Keep an eye on what's moving and what's not. You don't want to be stuck with a warehouse full of last season's trends.

When you combine efficient delivery systems with savvy inventory management, you create a powerhouse operation. Customers get their products on time, and you keep your cash flow healthy. It's a win-win!

But let's not forget about the human element. Have you ever had a shipping issue and reached out to customer service? If they're friendly and helpful, you're more likely to forgive a hiccup. If they're rude or unhelpful? Forget it! You're out the door faster than a cat on a hot tin roof.

So, invest in training your team. Make sure they understand the importance of customer service in logistics. Encourage them to go above and beyond. A little kindness can turn a frustrated customer into a loyal one.

To wrap it all up, here's a quick checklist to ensure your logistics and supply chain are running like a well-oiled machine:

- Evaluate Your Delivery Options: Know your strengths and weaknesses.
- Invest in Technology: Use software to streamline processes.
- Train Your Team: Customer service is key.
- Monitor Inventory: Stay ahead of demand.
- Gather Feedback: Ask customers about their delivery experience.

Now, take a moment and think about your own business. Are you ready to take your logistics and supply chain to the next level? It's not just about moving products; it's about creating an experience that leaves customers saying, "Wow, that was easy!"

So, roll up your sleeves, dive in, and make logistics your secret weapon in the quest for global market reach. You got this!

Chapter 10

Harness the power of tech

Alright, let's roll up our sleeves and jump into the fascinating world of technology, shall we? You know, that incredible place where everything seems to glide along like butter on warm toast? Seriously, it's not just some fancy term tossed around at dinner parties or in board meetings. Nope, technology is a total game-changer for businesses, especially if you're aiming to snag a billion buyers. Trust me, if you want to make that happen, you've got to harness the power of tech.

So, let's kick things off by talking about how tech can streamline operations. Picture this: you're trying to run a marathon in flip-flops. Sounds pretty rough, right? Well, that's pretty much what it feels like for businesses that aren't using technology to their advantage. From managing inventory to providing top-notch customer service, tech tools can really help smooth out those bumpy patches. Think about automation tools they can take care of all those repetitive tasks, like processing orders or responding to emails. This gives your team the freedom to focus on what really matters, like crafting that amazing marketing campaign or, hey, taking a well-deserved coffee break.

But hold on, it's not just about making life easier for you and your team; it's also about enhancing the experiences of your customers. Let's take a moment to think about it. When you walk into a store and the staff recognizes you by name, knows your favorite products, and even remembers your birthday how does that make you feel? Pretty special, right? That's the kind of magic technology can create. By utilizing customer relationship management (CRM) systems, businesses can keep track of interactions and preferences. This means you can offer personalized recommendations, turning a casual shopper into a loyal fan. And who doesn't want that kind of loyalty?

Now, let's sprinkle in a little data analytics. You might be thinking, "Why should I care about numbers?" Well, let me tell you, numbers can tell a pretty compelling story. They can reveal buying patterns and preferences that you might not have even considered before. Imagine having a crystal ball that shows you exactly what your customers want. With data analytics, you can dive into past purchases, website interactions, and even social media engagement to predict future behavior. It's like being a business psychic, minus the crystal ball and those questionable wardrobe choices.

Here's a fun little story for you. A buddy of mine runs a small online store that specializes in artisanal hot sauces. When he first started out, he was kind of like a chef throwing spaghetti at the wall to see what stuck he had no clue who his customers were or what they wanted. But once he started using data analytics, everything changed. He discovered that his best-selling sauce was a smoky chipotle blend. Armed with that knowledge, he launched a marketing campaign focused on that flavor, and guess what? Sales skyrocketed. The lesson here? Data isn't just for math geeks; it's a treasure trove for savvy business owners.

Alright, let's shift gears and chat about some of the innovative tools out there, like virtual reality (VR). If you're not familiar with VR, think of it as a magical portal that transports customers right into your product experience. For example, if you're selling furniture, VR can allow potential buyers to "walk" through a virtual room filled with your pieces. They can see how that sleek coffee table fits into their living room without ever leaving their couch. It's like giving them a sneak peek into their future life who wouldn't want that?

But wait a minute VR isn't just for the big players in the game. Small businesses can jump in on the action too! There are affordable VR platforms that let you create immersive experiences without emptying your wallet. Plus, the novelty of VR can really set you apart from your competitors. When was the last time you saw a local shop offering a virtual tour? Exactly. You'd be the talk of the town!

Now, I can already hear you thinking, "This all sounds great, but how do I actually implement these technologies?" Don't worry, I've got you covered with a handy-dandy list to help you get started:

1. Identify your pain points: Take a good look at your business and figure out what areas could use a little tech magic. Are there tasks that take too long? Is customer service lacking? Pinpoint those spots.

2. Research available tools: Dive into the world of software and platforms that fit your needs and budget. There are tons of options out there, so take your time to find the right fit.

3. Start small: You don't have to overhaul your entire operation overnight. Pick one tool to implement at a time and see how it goes. Baby steps, my friend.

4. Train your team: Make sure everyone knows how to use the new tech. A well-trained team is a happy team! Plus, it'll save you headaches down the line.

5. Measure your results: Keep an eye on how these changes impact your business. Are you saving time? Are customers happier? Adjust as needed based on what you find.

And here's a little nugget of wisdom: don't be afraid to experiment. Technology is always evolving, and what works today might not work tomorrow. Stay curious and be willing to adapt.

So, what's the takeaway here? Technology is your friend. It can streamline operations, enhance customer experiences, and provide valuable insights into buying patterns. Plus, with innovative tools like VR, you can create unforgettable interactions with your products. It's a win-win, folks.

Now, let's dive a bit deeper into the emotional side of things. Think about how technology has transformed our lives not just in business, but in everyday moments. Remember when you used to have to go to the library to look up information? Now, with just a few taps on your smartphone, you can access a world of knowledge. It's kind of mind-blowing, isn't it?

And let's not forget about the way technology connects us. Ever had a heartwarming moment when you video-called a friend or family member who lives halfway across the world? That feeling of seeing their smile and hearing their laughter, even though a screen, is something special. It's like technology has shrunk the world, making it easier to stay close to the people we care about, no matter the distance.

But, of course, it's not all sunshine and rainbows. There are challenges that come with the rapid pace of technological change. Sometimes it feels overwhelming, right? New tools and platforms pop up almost daily, and keeping up can feel like trying to catch a greased pig. You might find yourself asking, "Am I even doing this right?" It's totally normal to feel a bit lost in the sea of options.

That's why it's so important to take a step back and remember why you're embracing technology in the first place. It's not just about keeping up with the latest trends; it's about enhancing your business and creating a better experience for your customers. Focus on the big picture, and don't get bogged down by the little details.

Let's take a moment to think about the human side of technology. Sure, it's easy to get caught up in the numbers and the tools, but at the end of the day, it's all about people. Your customers are real human beings with feelings, desires, and needs. Technology can help you understand them better, but it's the personal touch that truly makes a difference.

Imagine a customer walks into your store, and you greet them with a warm smile. You remember their last purchase and ask how they liked it. That little bit of personal attention can go a long way. Technology can help you gather the information to make those connections, but it's your genuine interest that will keep them coming back.

Now, let's circle back to that list I gave you earlier. Implementing technology is a journey, not a race. It's okay to take your time and find what works best for you. You might hit a few bumps along the way, but that's all part of the process. Embrace the learning experience, and don't be afraid to ask for help when you need it. There's a whole community out there of business owners and tech enthusiasts who are more than willing to share their insights.

And speaking of community, let's not overlook the power of collaboration. Sometimes, partnering with other businesses can open up new doors. Maybe there's a local tech startup that can help you with your digital marketing, or perhaps you can team up with another small business to host a joint event. The possibilities are endless!

So, what's the bottom line? Technology isn't just a tool; it's a bridge that connects you to your customers, enhances your operations, and helps you grow your business. It's about finding the right balance between leveraging tech and maintaining that human touch.

As you navigate this tech landscape, keep in mind that it's all about progress, not perfection. Celebrate the small wins along the way, whether it's successfully implementing a new tool or receiving positive feedback from a customer. Those little victories will keep you motivated and remind you why you started this journey in the first place.

Now, let's wrap this up with a little encouragement. You've got this! Embrace the tools at your disposal, and watch your business transform into a powerhouse ready to attract those one billion buyers. And remember, if you ever feel overwhelmed, just think of it like riding a bike. You might wobble a bit at first, but once you find your balance, you'll be cruising down the road in no time.

So go forth, my friend! Dive headfirst into the world of technology, and let it elevate your business to new heights. You're not just a business owner; you're a trailblazer, ready to conquer the tech landscape and create meaningful connections with your customers. And who knows? You might just inspire others to do the same.

Chapter 11

Navigating Regulations

Let's talk about regulations, shall we? Now, I know what you're thinking: "Regulations? Yawn!" But hang on a second! These aren't just boring rules; they're the backbone of how you'll operate your business in different countries. Think of regulations as the road signs on your entrepreneurial journey. Ignore them, and you might just find yourself driving straight into a brick wall.

Every country has its own set of laws that dictate how businesses can operate. It's like trying to play a game of Monopoly with a bunch of different rulebooks. One country might let you buy Boardwalk with just $200, while another might have you pay double rent just for landing on it! Confusing, right?

So, what do you do? You need to get your hands dirty and dive into the nitty-gritty of these regulations. Yes, it's tedious. Yes, it takes time. But trust me, it's worth it. You don't want to be that business owner who gets slapped with hefty fines or, worse, gets shut down because you didn't comply with local laws.

Now, let's talk about trade agreements. These bad boys can be your best friends when it comes to expanding your market reach and cutting costs. Picture this: you've got a hot new product that everyone wants, but the shipping fees to get it overseas are sky-high. Enter trade agreements! These are like VIP passes that let you skip the long lines and save a few bucks along the way. They can reduce tariffs, making it cheaper for you to import and export goods.

You might be wondering, "How do I even find out about these agreements?" Well, start with a little research. Websites like the Office of the United States Trade Representative (USTR) can provide you with a treasure trove of information. Or better yet, connect with a trade expert who can help you navigate the complex world of international trade.

Now, here's where it gets real: complying with local regulations isn't just about avoiding fines; it's about building trust with your customers. When you show that you respect their laws and culture, you're not just a faceless business; you become a part of the community. And trust me, people like to buy from businesses they trust. It's like that old saying, "You catch more flies with honey than vinegar."

So, how do you ensure compliance? Start by creating a checklist of local regulations you need to adhere to. This could include things like labeling requirements, import/export restrictions, and even labor laws. Break it down into bite-sized pieces so it doesn't feel overwhelming.

Here's a quick action plan to get you started:

1. Research the regulations in your target market.
2. Create a compliance checklist tailored to those regulations.
3. Consult with local legal experts to clarify any gray areas.
4. Regularly review and update your checklist as laws change.
5. Build relationships with local authorities to stay informed.

Now, I get it. This might sound like a lot of work, but think of it as an investment in your business. It's like putting on a seatbelt before you hit the road. Sure, it takes a few seconds, but it could save your life or in this case, your business.

And hey, if you're feeling a little overwhelmed, don't worry! We've all been there. I remember when I first tried to expand my business overseas. I was knee-deep in regulations, trade agreements, and compliance checklists. I felt like I was drowning in a sea of legal jargon. But once I broke it down into manageable chunks, it all started to make sense.

You've got this! Embrace the challenge, and soon enough, you'll be navigating regulations like a pro. And when you do, you'll find that your business can flourish in ways you never thought possible.

So, let's wrap this up with a little pep talk. Regulations might seem like a hassle, but they're your roadmap to success in the global market. By understanding the laws, leveraging trade agreements, and complying with local regulations, you'll not only avoid legal pitfalls but also build a strong foundation for your business.

Now go out there and conquer the world one regulation at a time!

Chapter 12

Building relationships with other businesses

Let's dive into something that can seriously make or break your business: networking. Yeah, I know when you hear the word "networking," it can feel like you're stepping into a world of buzzwords and clichés, especially at those big conferences where everyone seems to be wearing their best "I'm super important" face. But trust me, this isn't just some corporate jargon; it's the real deal. Building relationships with other businesses isn't just a nice-to-have it's an absolute must if you want to grow and thrive in today's competitive landscape.

Think of networking like planting a garden. You can't just toss some seeds in the dirt and hope for the best, right? You've got to nurture those relationships, water them, give them sunlight, and, well, a little love to see them bloom into new opportunities. I mean, who doesn't want a garden full of possibilities?

I still remember my first foray into the business world. Picture this: I walked into my first networking event feeling like a deer caught in headlights. Seriously, I was standing there, clutching it like it was a life preserver in a sea of unfamiliar faces. My heart was racing, and I thought, "What am I even doing here?" But then, something amazing happened. I struck up a conversation with a local entrepreneur someone who'd been around the block a few times. She shared her journey, her struggles, and her successes, and I was, well, kinda shocked by how much I learned in just a short chat. That conversation opened my eyes to the power of connections. I walked away not just with a business card but with a potential partnership that would help me navigate the choppy waters of starting my new venture.

So, how do you go about building these valuable relationships? Here are some practical tips to help you get started. And hey, these aren't just your run-of-the-mill suggestions; they're things that have worked for me and could work for you too.

First off, be authentic. I can't stress this enough. People can smell insincerity from a mile away. If you're just approaching someone because you want something from them, they'll pick up on that vibe faster than you can say "networking." Instead, be genuinely interested in what they do. Ask questions, listen actively, and engage in meaningful conversations. You'd be surprised how far a little authenticity can go.

Next up, find local allies. Teaming up with businesses in your area can be a game-changer. If you're a tech startup looking to branch out into a new city, why not partner with a local business that knows the lay of the land? They can offer insights that you'd never find in a textbook, and it's a great way to support the local economy. Plus, it just feels good to be part of a community, doesn't it?

And let's not forget about attending networking events. Seriously, these gatherings can be goldmines for valuable connections and insights. I remember attending a local chamber of commerce event that felt like stepping into a treasure trove of knowledge. I met industry leaders, learned about upcoming trends, and even found a mentor who's been a guiding light for me ever since. The best part? You never know who you'll meet. That quiet guy in the corner? He could be the next big thing, just waiting for the right conversation to spark his journey.

Now, here's a tip that might seem simple but is super important: follow up. After you meet someone, don't just let that connection fizzle out like a soda left open too long. Shoot them a quick email or connect with them on LinkedIn. A simple "Hey, it was great chatting with you!" can go a long way. It shows that you value the connection and are interested in keeping the conversation going. Trust me, it makes a difference.

Speaking of connections, let's talk about leveraging social media. Platforms like LinkedIn are perfect for networking. Share articles, comment on posts, and engage with others in your industry. It's a great way to showcase your expertise and attract like-minded professionals. And hey, it doesn't have to be all serious business talk. A little humor or a personal touch can make your posts stand out in a sea of corporate chatter.

Now, here's a little secret: be a resource. Offer help before asking for it. If you know someone who could benefit from a connection, make that introduction. If you've got valuable insights, share them. When you're seen as a resource, people are more likely to return the favor. It's all about building that reciprocity, you know?

Let's shift gears for a second and talk about the benefits of these partnerships. Collaborating with other businesses can create a ripple effect of growth. When you pool resources, you not only expand your reach but also share knowledge and expertise. For example, if you're a small business owner, teaming up with a local marketing agency can help you navigate the tricky waters of digital advertising. They've got the know-how, and you've got the local insights. It's a win-win situation, and who doesn't love those?

And don't underestimate the insights you can gain from networking events. These gatherings are often filled with industry experts who are eager to share their experiences. I once attended a panel discussion where a successful entrepreneur shared their journey through a major market shift. It was like a lightbulb moment for me. I realized that the challenges I faced weren't unique, and there were strategies I could implement to adapt. It was comforting to know I wasn't alone in my struggles.

But let's be real for a second networking can be downright intimidating. You might feel like you're walking into a room full of sharks while you're just a little fish trying to find your way. But here's the thing: everyone else is there for the same reason to connect and grow. So, take a deep breath, put on your best smile, and dive in. You've got this!

And if you ever find yourself in a situation where you're unsure of what to say, just ask questions. People love talking about themselves and their businesses. It's like free therapy! Plus, you'll learn a ton in the process. You'll be surprised how many people are willing to share their stories and insights if you just give them the chance.

In summary, building relationships with other businesses can create new opportunities for growth. Collaborating with local companies can help you navigate new markets more effectively, and networking events can provide valuable connections and insights into industry trends. So, get out there, make those connections, and watch your business flourish.

Now, here's a little challenge for you: attend at least one networking event this month. Set a goal to meet three new people and follow up with them afterward. You never know where those connections might lead. Maybe you'll find a mentor, a partner, or even a friend.

And remember, it's not just about what you can get; it's about what you can give. So, be a connector, be a resource, and watch your network grow. It's a beautiful thing, really. You'll find that the more you invest in others, the more it comes back to you in unexpected ways.

Now, let's take a moment to talk about some of the emotions that come with networking. It's not all sunshine and rainbows, right?

Sometimes, you might feel overwhelmed or anxious about putting yourself out there. That's completely normal! I mean, who hasn't felt that little knot in their stomach before walking into a room full of strangers? But here's the thing: those feelings are part of the journey. Embrace them! They're a sign that you're stepping out of your comfort zone, and that's where the magic happens.

I remember one particular event where I felt like I was going to throw up from nerves. I almost turned around and left. But then I took a deep breath, reminded myself of my goals, and walked in anyway. I ended up having some fantastic conversations and even met someone who would later become a key collaborator on a project I was passionate about. It's funny how often we let fear hold us back from amazing opportunities. So, if you're feeling that way, just know you're not alone. Everyone else is feeling something similar, even if they're putting on a brave face.

Now, let's talk about the importance of diversity in your network. It's so easy to gravitate toward people who are just like you same industry, same background, same experiences. But if you want to grow, you need to step outside that bubble. Seek out people with different perspectives, experiences, and expertise. It's like adding new colors to your palette. You'll find that the more diverse your network, the richer your insights and opportunities will be.

And speaking of diversity, let's not forget about the power of mentorship. Finding a mentor can be a game-changer for your career. It's like having a personal guide who's been there, done that, and can help you navigate the twists and turns of your journey. I've been fortunate enough to have a few mentors who have offered invaluable advice and support. They've helped me see things from different angles and encouraged me to take risks I might not have considered on my own. So, don't hesitate to seek out mentors in your network. You might be surprised at how willing people are to help if you just ask.

Now, let's circle back to the idea of giving back. As you build your network, remember that it's not just about what you can gain; it's about what you can contribute. Share your knowledge, offer your expertise, and help others when you can. It's like planting seeds of goodwill that will eventually come back to you in unexpected ways. Plus, it just feels good to be a resource for others. It creates a sense of community and connection that can be incredibly rewarding.

And don't forget to celebrate your wins, no matter how small. Every connection you make, every meaningful conversation you have, is a step forward. Take a moment to acknowledge those victories. It'll keep you motivated and remind you of why you're putting yourself out there in the first place.

So, as you embark on your networking journey, remember to be authentic, seek out diverse connections, and give back whenever you can. Embrace the emotions that come with it, and don't shy away from the challenges. You're building a network that can support you, inspire you, and help you grow in ways you might not even imagine right now.

Now, let's wrap this up with a little action plan. Start by setting a goal for yourself. Maybe it's attending that networking event you've been putting off, or reaching out to someone you admire in your industry. Whatever it is, take that first step. You'll be amazed at how much your confidence will grow as you start to put yourself out there.

And remember, networking isn't a one-time thing. It's an ongoing process. Keep nurturing those relationships, and don't be afraid to reach out and reconnect with people down the line. You never know when an old connection might lead to a new opportunity.

So, go ahead get out there, make those connections, and watch your business flourish. You've got this! And who knows? You might just find that the journey of networking is just as rewarding as the destination itself. Happy connecting!

Chapter 13

Personalization in Marketing

Let's dive into the world of personalization in marketing. Now, if you're thinking, "What's the big deal?" Well, my friend, buckle up. This is where the magic happens. Tailoring products and advertisements to individual preferences isn't just a nice-to-have; it's a MUST-HAVE if you want to boost sales and keep customers coming back for more.

Think about it. When was the last time, you felt like a brand truly understood you? Maybe it was that time you received an email suggesting that perfect pair of shoes to match your new dress. Or perhaps it was a personalized recommendation on Netflix that had you binge-watching until the wee hours. That's the power of personalization, folks. It's like having a personal shopper who knows your taste better than your best friend.

So, how do we make this happen? Let's break it down into bite-sized pieces.

1. Know Your Audience: Start by gathering data on your customers. Who are they? What do they like? What do they need? Use surveys, social media insights, and website analytics to create a detailed profile of your target audience. The more you know, the better you can tailor your offerings.

2. Segment Your Customers: Not all customers are created equal. Some are bargain hunters, while others are willing to splurge on luxury items. Segment your audience based on their behaviors and preferences. This allows you to craft messages that resonate with each group.

3. Craft Personalized Messages: Once you've got your segments, it's time to get creative. Personalized emails and targeted ads can make customers feel valued. Use their names, reference their past purchases, and suggest products that align with their interests. You wouldn't send a vegan a steak ad, right?

4. Utilize Technology: There are tons of tools out there to help you personalize your marketing. Customer Relationship Management (CRM) systems can track customer interactions and preferences, while AI can analyze data to predict future behaviors. Think of it as

having a crystal ball that tells you what your customers want before they even know it themselves.

5. Respect Customer Data: Here's the kicker using customer data responsibly is crucial. People are more likely to engage with your brand if they feel their information is safe. Be transparent about how you collect and use data. If you promise to keep it secure, make sure you deliver. Trust is the name of the game.

Now, let's talk about the benefits of personalization. It's not just about making customers feel warm and fuzzy inside (though that's a nice bonus). Personalized marketing can lead to higher conversion rates, increased customer loyalty, and ultimately, a boost in sales. According to a study by Epsilon, 80% of consumers are more likely to make a purchase when brands offer personalized experiences. That's a statistic worth writing home about!

But don't just take my word for it. Let me share a little story from my own experience. A few years back, I was working with a small online retailer that sold handmade jewelry. They were struggling to connect with their audience. We decided to revamp their email marketing strategy. Instead of sending out generic newsletters, we segmented their customer base and sent tailored emails based on past purchases and browsing behavior. The result? A 30% increase in click-through rates and a significant boost in sales. People loved feeling like they were getting special treatment.

But wait, there's more! Personalization doesn't stop at emails and ads. You can also tailor the shopping experience on your website. Consider implementing product recommendations based on browsing history. If someone is checking out yoga mats, why not suggest a stylish water bottle or a set of resistance bands? It's like being a helpful friend who knows just what you need.

And let's not forget about the power of social media. Platforms like Facebook and Instagram allow for highly targeted advertising. You can reach users based on their interests, behaviors, and even their demographics. If you're selling eco-friendly products, target users who have shown interest in sustainability. It's all about being smart with your approach.

Now, I know what you might be thinking: "Isn't personalization just a bit creepy?" It's a valid concern. But here's the thing when done right, personalization enhances the customer experience. It's about creating a connection, not stalking them. Think of it as being the thoughtful friend who remembers your favorite coffee order, not the weird guy who shows up at your door uninvited.

So, what's the takeaway here? Personalization in marketing isn't just a trend; it's a powerful strategy that can transform your business. By tailoring products and advertisements to individual preferences, you can boost sales, foster customer loyalty, and create a shopping experience that feels personal and valued.

As you move forward, remember these key points:

- Know your audience inside and out.
- Segment your customers for targeted messaging.
- Use technology to your advantage while respecting privacy.
- Personalize every touchpoint, from emails to website experiences.

Now, I challenge you to take a step back and assess your current marketing strategies. Are you personalizing your approach? If not, it's time to roll up your sleeves and get to work. Your customers are waiting for that special touch that only you can provide. So go ahead, make them feel valued, and watch your sales soar.

Chapter 14

Understanding Economic Trends: Your Secret Weapon.

You know, understanding economic trends is a bit like trying to read the room at a party. One moment, everything feels upbeat and lively, and then just like that someone mentions politics, and suddenly, the vibe shifts. In the business world, those shifts can feel just as abrupt. One day, you're riding high, feeling confident about your sales, and the next day BAM! The economy takes a nosedive, and your customers are nowhere to be found. It's enough to make anyone's heart race, right? But don't worry too much. Getting a handle on these economic trends can be your secret weapon, your ace in the hole, in the ever-evolving game of global markets.

Let's kick things off by diving into spending habits. Imagine people's wallets as a pair of skinny jeans after a Thanksgiving feast tightening up in a hurry! When the economy is booming, people are more likely to splurge on that shiny new gadget or book that spontaneous weekend getaway. But when things get shaky like during a recession those same folks might think twice before pulling out their credit cards. Keeping your finger on the pulse of these economic shifts is crucial.

So, how do you keep track of all this? Well, think of it as having your own personal crystal ball for your business. It's not just about staring at stock market tickers and hoping for the best. You've got to look at the bigger picture. For instance, if you notice a country's GDP is on the rise, that's a pretty good sign that people might be feeling a little more generous with their wallets. On the flip side, if unemployment rates are creeping up, you might want to hit the brakes on that new luxury line you've been dreaming about.

Now, I can almost hear you thinking, "But how do I actually keep track of all this?" Here's a little insider tip subscribe to economic newsletters or follow financial analysts on social media. Seriously, platforms like Bloomberg and The Economist are like treasure troves of insights just waiting for you to dig in. And if you want to be super proactive, set up Google Alerts for specific economic indicators that matter to your business. That way, you'll be the first to know when something shifts, and you can react accordingly.

Adapting to economic conditions isn't just a nice-to-have; it's a MUST-HAVE if you want to stay competitive. Picture it like a game of chess. If your opponent makes a move, you've got to be ready to respond. If you notice a dip in consumer spending, maybe it's time to pivot your marketing strategy. You could offer discounts, create bundles, or even explore that subscription model everyone seems to be raving about these days.

Let me share a little story. I had a friend who owned a small bakery. When the economy took a hit, she noticed fewer customers were popping in for those extravagant cakes she was famous for. Instead of sulking in the corner, she decided to adapt. She started offering smaller, more affordable treats and even introduced a "bake-at-home" kit that customers could take home and enjoy. And guess what? Sales skyrocketed! She didn't just survive the downturn; she thrived. That's the power of being flexible and responsive to economic changes.

Now, let's break it down a bit. Here's a quick rundown of how you can stay ahead of the curve in this unpredictable economic landscape:

1. Monitor Economic Indicators: Keep tabs on GDP, unemployment rates, and consumer confidence. These numbers are

like the heartbeat of the economy, and knowing how they're doing can give you a heads-up on what to expect.

2. Subscribe to Economic News: Getting insights from reliable sources can help you anticipate market shifts. It's like having a backstage pass to the economic show.

3. Be Flexible: Don't be afraid to pivot your strategy based on what the economy is telling you. If you notice a trend, jump on it! Adaptability is key.

4. Innovate: Look for new ways to meet consumer needs, especially during tough times. Think outside the box and don't shy away from trying something new.

5. Network: Connect with other business owners to share insights and strategies. There's power in community, and you might just pick up a tip or two that can help you navigate the waters.

Now, let's take a moment to talk about the emotional side of this whole thing. I mean, it's easy to get caught up in the numbers and the strategies, but there's a real human element here. When the economy takes a turn for the worse, it can feel personal. You might worry about your employees, your customers, and the impact on your community. It's okay to feel that weight. It's a lot to carry. But remember, you're not alone in this. We're all in this together, navigating the wild world of global commerce one economic trend at a time.

So, take a deep breath. You've got this. Stay informed, stay adaptable, and keep your eyes peeled for opportunities. If you can do that, you'll not only survive but potentially even come out stronger on the other side. And if you've got questions or need a little encouragement along the way, don't hesitate to reach out. We're all just trying to make sense of this crazy economic dance together.

Now, let's dive a little deeper into some of these strategies. Monitoring economic indicators is more than just a numbers game; it's about understanding the stories behind those numbers. For instance, when you see GDP rising, it's not just a statistic it's a signal that people are feeling more secure in their jobs and finances. That's when they're likely to spend a little more on that fancy dinner or that new outfit.

On the flip side, when unemployment rates are climbing, it tells a different story. People are tightening their belts, and that's when you might want to think about how to adjust your offerings. Maybe it's time to introduce budget-friendly options or emphasize value in your marketing.

And let's not forget about consumer confidence. It's like a mood ring for the economy. When confidence is high, people are more willing to spend. But when it dips, you'll want to pay attention. It's a good time to think about how you can reassure your customers and provide them with the value they're looking for.

Speaking of reassurance, that brings us to the importance of communication. During uncertain times, keeping the lines of communication open with your customers is crucial. Share updates about your business, any changes you're making, and how you're responding to the economic climate. Transparency builds trust, and trust is everything in business.

And let's chat a bit about innovation. This is where the magic happens. When the going gets tough, the tough get creative. Think about how you can innovate your products or services to meet changing consumer needs. Maybe it's offering virtual experiences, creating new product lines, or even collaborating with other businesses to offer unique packages. The possibilities are endless if you're willing to think outside the box.

Now, I know it can be overwhelming at times. The economic landscape is constantly shifting, and it's easy to feel like you're on a rollercoaster ride. But here's the thing: every challenge is also an opportunity. Those tough times can spark your creativity and lead you to discover new avenues for growth that you might not have considered otherwise.

Let's take another example. Think about the restaurant industry during the pandemic. Many restaurants faced unprecedented challenges, but some of them adapted brilliantly. They pivoted to takeout and delivery, created meal kits, and even started selling groceries. Those who were willing to innovate and adapt not only survived but found new ways to thrive in a challenging environment.

So, as you navigate the ever-changing rhythms of the economy, keep that spirit of innovation alive. Embrace change, and don't be afraid to experiment. You might just stumble upon the next big thing for your business.

And remember, it's okay to lean on your network during these times. Connect with other business owners, share your experiences, and learn from one another. You're not in this alone, and there's strength in community.

In closing, I want to emphasize that understanding economic trends is not just about crunching numbers or following the news. It's about being in tune with the world around you and being ready to adapt. It's about staying informed, being flexible, and embracing the opportunities that come your way.

So, take a deep breath, keep your eyes open, and get ready to dance with the ever-changing rhythms of the economy. If you can do that, you'll not only navigate the ups and downs but also find ways to thrive. And hey, if you ever feel lost or need a little nudge in the right direction, reach out. We're all in this together, and together, we can tackle whatever the economy throws our way.

Chapter 15

The Future of Global Commerce

Hey there! Let's chat about something that's been on my mind lately the future of global commerce. You know, it's a bit like watching a really good movie where the plot twists keep coming. Just when you think you've got it figured out, bam! Something new pops up and changes everything. It's wild, really. Emerging technologies are shaking things up in ways that feel both exciting and a little bit daunting. I mean, it's like that moment when you realize your grandma's flip phone just can't keep up with the latest iPhone. You get what I'm saying?

We're talking about game-changers like AI, blockchain, and all that jazz. These aren't just fancy buzzwords that tech geeks throw around; they're actually reshaping how businesses operate in ways we couldn't have imagined just a decade ago. And let me tell you, if you're not paying attention, you might find yourself left in the dust, wondering what the heck happened. So, grab a cup of coffee (or tea, no judgment here), and let's dive into what's happening in this crazy world of commerce and how you can ride this wave of change.

First off, let's break down what **AI** and blockchain really mean for you. Artificial Intelligence, or **AI** for short, is like having a super-smart assistant who never sleeps. Seriously, this thing can analyze data faster than you can say "e-commerce." It helps businesses understand customer behavior and preferences in a way that feels almost magical. Imagine a world where your marketing strategies are tailored to each individual based on their past purchases and browsing habits. It's like Netflix recommendations but for everything you buy! Sounds pretty futuristic, right? Well, guess what? It's happening right now, and if you're not on board, you might just miss out on some serious opportunities.

Now, let's talk about blockchain. This one's a bit of a buzzword too, but it's actually pretty cool. Think of blockchain as a digital ledger that's transparent and secure. It's like a high-tech diary that everyone can see, but no one can tamper with. This technology can streamline transactions, reduce fraud, and even improve supply chain transparency. Imagine being able to track a product from its origin to your doorstep, knowing exactly where it's been and how it got there. It's the kind of tech that can make your business not just more efficient, but also more trustworthy in the eyes of consumers.

And let's be real trust is the currency of the digital age. If your customers don't trust you, good luck getting them to hit that "buy now" button.

So, why should you care about these trends? Well, understanding future trends can help you prepare for upcoming challenges. It's like getting a sneak peek at the next season of your favorite show. If you know what's coming, you can strategize and position yourself to take advantage of new opportunities. You wouldn't want to be the last one to know that your favorite band is going on tour, right? You'd want to snag those tickets before they sell out! The same goes for your business. Staying ahead of the curve can mean the difference between thriving and just surviving.

Now, let's get into some of the future trends we should be keeping an eye on. Here's a quick rundown of what's on the horizon:

1. Personalization: Customers today expect a tailored experience. If you're not personalizing your marketing, you're missing the boat. Think about it those Netflix recommendations? They're working hard to keep you engaged. You should do the same for your audience. Whether it's sending personalized emails or

recommending products based on past purchases, making your customers feel special can go a long way.

2. Sustainability: Consumers are becoming more environmentally conscious. They want to know that their purchases are making a positive impact. If your business isn't adopting sustainable practices, you might find yourself in hot water. It's not just a trend; it's a movement. People want to support brands that care about the planet, so if you're not on board, you might want to rethink your strategy.

3. Omni-channel shopping: Customers are shopping across multiple platforms. They might start on their phone, browse on their laptop, and then finalize the purchase in-store. You need to be everywhere they are. If you're not offering a seamless shopping experience across all channels, you could lose out on potential sales. It's all about meeting your customers where they are, and that means being present on various platforms.

4. Remote work: This isn't just a trend; it's a shift in how we do business. Embrace it! Flexible work arrangements can lead to happier employees and increased productivity. Plus, it opens up a wider talent pool. You're not just limited to hiring people in your

city anymore. The world is your oyster, and you can find the best talent, no matter where they are.

5. Social commerce: Social media isn't just for scrolling anymore; it's a shopping platform. If you're not leveraging social media to sell your products, you're missing a huge opportunity. Platforms like Instagram and Facebook are becoming increasingly integrated with e-commerce, and you should definitely take advantage of that. It's all about meeting your customers where they're hanging out online.

Now that we've covered some trends, let's talk about how to stay informed and ready for these changes. You've got to be proactive. Here are some actionable steps you can take to stay ahead of the game:

- Follow industry news: Subscribe to newsletters, podcasts, and blogs that focus on global commerce and technology. The more informed you are, the better decisions you can make. Knowledge is power, after all.

- Network with experts: Attend conferences, webinars, and workshops. You'll meet people who are at the forefront of these changes and can share insights that you won't find in textbooks.

Plus, it's a great way to make connections and maybe even find some mentors along the way.

- Experiment with new technologies: Don't be afraid to try out new tools and platforms. Whether it's AI-driven analytics or blockchain for transactions, get your hands dirty. You'll learn more by doing than by just reading. And who knows? You might discover something that completely transforms your business.

- Invest in training: Encourage your team to learn about emerging technologies. Consider online courses or certifications. A well-informed team is an asset that can drive your business forward. Plus, it shows your employees that you value their growth, which can lead to higher job satisfaction.

- Adapt and evolve: Be willing to pivot your strategies based on what you learn. The business landscape is changing rapidly, and flexibility can be your best friend. If something isn't working, don't be afraid to change course. It's all part of the game.

So, what's the takeaway here? Global commerce is evolving, and if you want to stay ahead, you need to stay informed. Embrace these technologies and trends, and don't shy away from new opportunities. It's a wild world out there, but with the right tools and mindset, you can navigate it like a pro.

Now, let's get real for a second. I remember when I first started my journey in e-commerce. I was like a kid in a candy store, overwhelmed by choices but excited about possibilities. It was exhilarating, but I also made my fair share of mistakes, believe me. Each misstep taught me something valuable, though. I learned to embrace change, to adapt quickly, and to never underestimate the power of technology.

I'll never forget this one time I launched a product without fully understanding my target audience. Spoiler alert: it flopped. Hard. But that failure pushed me to dive deeper into market research and customer feedback. I learned that understanding your audience isn't just a checkbox; it's a vital part of your strategy. And now, I can't imagine launching anything without first gathering insights. It's like trying to bake a cake without knowing the recipe you might end up with a disaster on your hands.

As you look to the future, remember that challenges will arise. But with every challenge comes an opportunity. Whether it's adopting AI to streamline your operations or leveraging blockchain for secure transactions, the possibilities are endless. The key is to stay curious and keep learning.

So, here's my challenge to you: Stay curious. Stay informed. And don't be afraid to embrace the unknown. The future of global commerce is bright for those who are willing to adapt and grow. Now, go out there and make it happen!

And hey, if you ever feel overwhelmed by it all, just remember that everyone starts somewhere. You don't have to have all the answers right away. It's a journey, and every step you take is part of the learning process. Keep your head up, keep pushing forward, and you'll find your way. The world is changing, and it's up to you to seize the opportunities that come your way. So, let's do this together!

Chapter 16

The Global Market.

Understanding the Billion-Buyer Vision

Definition of "buyers" in the digital age: In today's interconnected world, buyers are no longer confined to local markets. A "buyer" encompasses anyone who can be reached digitally or physically to purchase goods or services. This includes individual consumers, businesses, and even government entities participating in commerce. Buyers today are empowered by access to information, a variety of payment options, and the convenience of global shipping.

Key characteristics of a "good buyer": Good buyers are repeat customers who are willing to spend consistently. They exhibit loyalty, provide feedback, and often act as brand advocates. Characteristics include a willingness to pay for quality, openness to trying new products, and engagement with a brand's content and community. Identifying and nurturing good buyers is crucial for scaling globally.

Why the Billion-Buyer Goal Matters

Potential market size and revenue: Reaching one billion buyers opens doors to unprecedented revenue opportunities. This scale of engagement signifies a business's transition from regional success to a truly global presence. For example, if each buyer spends just $10 annually, the revenue potential would be $10 billion.

Transforming economies through global trade: The billion-buyer vision isn't just about revenue; it's also about making a transformative impact on global economies. Businesses that scale globally can help create jobs, improve infrastructure, and foster innovation in markets they enter. Additionally, consumers in emerging economies gain access to products and services previously unavailable to them.

The Evolution of Global Markets

Historical perspective: Global trade dates back centuries, from the Silk Road to colonial trade routes. However, the digital revolution has drastically accelerated globalization. With the rise of the internet, e-commerce platforms, and FinTech innovations, businesses can now connect with buyers in real-time, regardless of geographical barriers.

Digital globalization: Unlike traditional globalization, which often relied on physical infrastructure, digital globalization leverages technology. Companies like Amazon, Alibaba, and Shopify have democratized access to global markets, allowing even small businesses to think and act globally. This evolution has created a level playing field where the size of a business no longer dictates its potential reach.

Key Challenges in Reaching a Billion Buyers

Cultural diversity: Buyers from different regions have unique preferences, cultural norms, and buying behaviors. Understanding and respecting these differences is key to success. For example, marketing strategies that work in North America may need significant adaptation for Asian or African markets.

Logistical complexities: Shipping products across borders involves navigating tariffs, taxes, and varying postal systems. Efficient logistics solutions are necessary to ensure timely delivery and reduce costs, which are critical factors for buyer satisfaction.

Technological barriers: While technology has enabled global connectivity, disparities in internet access and digital literacy remain a challenge in certain regions. Bridging this gap requires innovative solutions, such as mobile-first strategies and partnerships with local tech providers.

Setting the Stage for the Billion-Buyer Journey

Visionary leadership: Achieving the billion-buyer goal requires leaders who can think big, act boldly, and adapt quickly. Visionary leaders set the tone for innovation, collaboration, and resilience within their organizations.

Collaborative ecosystems: No company can reach a billion buyers alone. Building partnerships with logistics providers, payment processors, and local market experts is essential. Collaboration fosters shared growth and helps overcome barriers more effectively. Commitment to continuous learning: The global market is dynamic, with trends shifting rapidly. Businesses must stay informed about emerging technologies, changing buyer preferences, and evolving regulatory landscapes to remain competitive.

This chapter establishes the foundation for understanding the immense potential and challenges of targeting a billion buyers. By embracing a global mindset and leveraging digital tools, businesses can unlock opportunities that were unimaginable just a few decades ago.

Chapter 17

Understanding the Buyer Demographics

Global Buyer Segments

Online buyers vs. offline buyers

Regional buying behaviors

Online Buyers vs. Offline Buyers

Understanding the distinction between online and offline buyers is critical for developing effective strategies.

Online Buyers:

Characteristics: Tech-savvy, value convenience, and often make purchases via mobile devices or computers.

Popular Categories: Electronics, fashion, groceries, and digital goods.

Key Platforms: E-commerce giants like Amazon, Alibaba, and regional platforms such as MercadoLibre (Latin America) and Flipkart (India).

Behavior Trends: Online buyers increasingly prefer personalized experiences, faster delivery options, and secure payment methods.

Offline Buyers:

Characteristics: Prefer physical interaction with products before purchasing, value in-store experiences, and tend to rely on traditional retail.

Popular Categories: Groceries, furniture, and certain luxury goods.

Regional Differences: Offline buying remains dominant in regions with limited internet access or cultural preferences for in-person shopping.

Regional Buying Behaviors

Regional differences significantly shape buyer behavior and preferences.

North America:

High internet penetration and disposable income drive e-commerce growth.

Buyers value convenience, same-day delivery, and seamless returns.

Popular Platforms: Amazon, Walmart, and eBay.

Europe:

Preferences vary between Western and Eastern Europe.

Western Europe: Strong emphasis on sustainability and ethical sourcing.

Eastern Europe: Growing interest in e-commerce as infrastructure improves.

Popular Platforms: Zalando, Shopify, and AliExpress.

Asia-Pacific:

The largest and fastest-growing e-commerce market globally.

Mobile-first buyers dominate, with significant demand for electronics, fashion, and beauty products.

Popular Platforms: Alibaba, JD.com, and Shopee.

Latin America:

Rapid adoption of online shopping due to improved internet access and mobile penetration.

Buyers prioritize affordability and local payment methods.

Popular Platforms: MercadoLibre and regional marketplaces.

Middle East & Africa:

Emerging markets with young populations driving e-commerce adoption.

Buyers seek affordable products and localized experiences.

Popular Platforms: Jumia, Noon, and Souq.

Cultural Influences:

Religion, traditions, and festivals play a significant role in shaping purchasing decisions.

Example: Peak buying seasons like Ramadan in the Middle East and Singles' Day in China.

Chapter 18

Identifying the Best Countries for Buyers

Top Countries for Online Buyers: Identifying the countries with the most promising markets for online buyers is essential for a billion-buyer strategy. Here are some critical factors that determine the suitability of a country:

E-commerce Penetration: Countries like the United States, China, and the United Kingdom have some of the highest e-commerce penetration rates. These regions have established infrastructure and buyer trust in online transactions.

Internet and Smartphone Access: High-speed internet and widespread smartphone usage are prerequisites for a strong online buyer base. Nations like South Korea and Japan lead in technology adoption, making them attractive markets.

GDP per Capita and Disposable Income: Wealthier nations, such as those in Western Europe and North America, have buyers with higher disposable incomes, which translates to greater spending power online.

Emerging Market Opportunities Emerging markets are the future of global commerce, offering untapped potential. Consider these key regions:

India: With over 1.4 billion people and growing internet penetration, India's e-commerce sector is expected to grow exponentially. The rise of platforms like Flipkart and Amazon India highlights the country's potential.

Southeast Asia: Countries like Indonesia, Vietnam, and Thailand are seeing rapid digital adoption. Mobile commerce is especially strong in this region, driven by a young and tech-savvy population.

Africa: While infrastructure challenges remain, nations such as Nigeria, Kenya, and South Africa are showing promise with increasing smartphone penetration and the rise of fintech solutions.

Region-Specific Insights To tailor strategies for success, it's crucial to understand regional preferences and challenges:

North America: Buyers in the U.S. and Canada value convenience and fast shipping. Platforms like Amazon dominate, but niche markets for artisanal and sustainable products are growing.

Europe: Europe is diverse, with significant differences between Western and Eastern regions. Western Europe prioritizes premium products and brand loyalty, while Eastern Europe offers opportunities in price-sensitive segments.

Asia-Pacific: The Asia-Pacific region is home to e-commerce giants like Alibaba and Tokopedia. Live-stream shopping and social commerce are gaining traction here.

Latin America: Brazil and Mexico lead the charge in online shopping, but logistics and payment challenges require innovative solutions.

Key Metrics to Evaluate a Market When assessing a country's potential, use these critical metrics:

Market Size: Number of internet users and online shoppers.

Growth Rate: Annual increase in e-commerce activity.

Logistics Performance: Ease of delivering goods across the region.

Cultural Compatibility: Alignment with your brand's values and product offerings.

Challenges to Consider Expanding globally isn't without hurdles:

Regulatory Complexity: Import/export restrictions, taxes, and data privacy laws vary by country.

Payment Preferences: Local payment methods, such as cash on delivery in some regions, need accommodation.

Competition: Established players and local startups can pose significant challenges.

By understanding these dynamics, businesses can strategically prioritize the best countries to target, maximizing their chances of success in reaching one billion buyers.

Chapter 19

The Digital Buyer Journey

Stages of the Buyer Funnel

Awareness: The first step in the buyer journey involves creating visibility. Businesses must ensure their product or service is discoverable through effective branding, advertising, and outreach campaigns.

Consideration: Once potential buyers are aware, they evaluate their options. This stage includes engaging content, social proof, testimonials, and detailed product information to guide decision-making.

Decision: Buyers commit to a purchase based on their confidence in the product. Key factors include pricing, promotional offers, and user-friendly checkout processes.

Loyalty: Retaining buyers through excellent post-purchase experiences is essential. Strategies include personalized follow-ups, loyalty programs, and exclusive offers.

Behavioral Insights

Global buyer behavior varies, but common motivations include value for money, quality, convenience, and trust.

B2B buyers focus on long-term reliability, bulk pricing, and post-sale support, while B2C buyers prioritize ease of use and immediate satisfaction.

Digital touchpoints, such as mobile apps, email campaigns, and social media, heavily influence buyer decisions.

Technology's Role in the Journey

Analytics tools help map buyer journeys and identify drop-off points.

Automation streamlines engagement, from chatbots for queries to automated reminders for cart recovery.

Chapter 20

Building a Billion-Buyer Strategy

Market Research Essentials

Understanding your audience: Use surveys, interviews, and analytics to identify buyer personas.

Competitive analysis: Study competitors' strengths, weaknesses, and strategies to uncover market gaps.

Trend analysis: Leverage tools like Google Trends, market reports, and social media insights to stay ahead.

Localization and Personalization

Language matters: Offering content and services in native languages increases accessibility and appeal.

Cultural customization: Adjust marketing strategies to align with local customs, values, and preferences.

Currency and payment options: Provide region-specific payment methods to remove barriers to purchase.

Scalability Tactics

Start local, think global: Test products in smaller, targeted regions before scaling internationally.

Strategic partnerships: Collaborate with local influencers, distributors, or platforms to build credibility.

Infrastructure investment: Ensure logistics, warehousing, and customer support are prepared for increased demand.

Customer-Centric Approach

Listen to feedback: Use reviews and surveys to understand buyer pain points and adapt accordingly.

Create a seamless experience: From website navigation to order tracking, prioritize user satisfaction.

Chapter 21

Leveraging Technology for Global Reach

E-commerce Platforms

Marketplace dominance: Platforms like Amazon, Alibaba, and Etsy provide access to millions of buyers but come with competition and fees.

Independent stores: Building a branded website offers control and differentiation, supported by tools like Shopify or Woo Commerce.

Mobile-first design: With a majority of buyers accessing platforms via smartphones, responsive and fast-loading sites are critical.

AI and Big Data

Predictive analytics: Analyze historical data to forecast demand, optimize inventory, and identify emerging trends.

Personalization engines: Use AI to offer tailored recommendations, dynamic pricing, and targeted ads.

Chabot and virtual assistants: Provide real-time support and enhance buyer satisfaction through conversational AI.

Payment Innovations

Digital wallets: Integrate options like PayPal, Apple Pay, and Google Pay to simplify checkout.

Cryptocurrency adoption: While niche, accepting crypto can attract tech-savvy buyers and early adopters.

Subscription models: Leverage recurring payments for steady revenue streams.

Logistics and Supply Chain Optimization

Smart warehousing: Use IoT and robotics to streamline operations and reduce errors.

Real-time tracking: Offer buyers visibility into their shipments through GPS-enabled logistics.

Sustainable practices: Implement eco-friendly packaging and carbon-neutral shipping options to appeal to conscious buyers.

Global Outreach Tools

Social media platforms: Use region-specific apps (e.g., WeChat in China, WhatsApp in India) for marketing and engagement.

Virtual and augmented reality: Enhance the shopping experience with VR showrooms or AR try-on features.

Cloud-based solutions: Leverage cloud technology to manage global operations efficiently.

Chapter 22

Digital Marketing for a Billion Buyers

Social Media Advertising.

Platforms with the largest user base.

In today's digital landscape, platforms like Facebook, Instagram, TikTok, WeChat, and YouTube are essential for global marketing. Each platform has millions of active users, providing an incredible opportunity to reach diverse buyer segments.

Facebook & Instagram: With over 3 billion users combined, these platforms allow precise targeting through demographics, interests, and behaviors.

TikTok: Popular among younger audiences, TikTok offers highly engaging, short-form video content that drives virality and global reach.

WeChat: The leading platform in China, WeChat's ecosystem covers everything from messaging to e-commerce.

YouTube: The largest video platform, essential for visual storytelling and educational content.

Twitter and LinkedIn: Particularly effective for B2B marketing and reaching professional audiences.

Effective Content Strategies

Content should align with the audience's preferences and cultural nuances.

Visual Storytelling: With a focus on short-form videos, interactive polls, and live streams, brands can create authentic connections.

Influencer Collaborations: Partnering with influencers can build credibility and accelerate brand awareness.

User-Generated Content: Encourage customers to share their experiences, which can amplify organic reach and trust.

Localized Content: Tailoring content to the local culture, language, and trends is crucial for success in different markets.

SEO and Content Marketing

Reaching International Audiences Organically

SEO is key to getting visibility in different countries without the need for paid ads.

Global Keyword Research: Identify search terms that international customers are using, considering local dialects and regional phrases.

International Link Building: Securing high-quality backlinks from authoritative websites in various countries boosts search rankings globally.

Localization: Localize website content, Meta tags, and images to ensure relevance in each market.

Importance of Multilingual SEO

Language Optimization: Ensure your website and content are optimized for multiple languages. Use reflag tags to signal to search engines which language version should be shown to users.

Cultural Sensitivity: Beyond translation, content should be culturally relevant, taking into account local customs, idioms, and preferences.

Chapter 23

Building Trust with Buyers

Importance of Brand Reputation

Strategies for Maintaining Credibility

In a billion-buyer market, reputation is everything. Brands must invest in building trust.

Customer Reviews & Testimonials: Encourage reviews across different platforms. Positive testimonials and user-generated content are powerful social proof.

Transparency: Clear messaging about the company's values, practices, and sourcing can build a loyal customer base.

Engagement: Direct interaction with customers through social media and customer service channels strengthens trust.

Overcoming Skepticism in New Markets

Entering new markets can be daunting, but by demonstrating value and authenticity, a brand can earn trust.

Partnerships with Local Influencers: Collaborating with local influencers who are trusted figures can help brands gain credibility quickly.

Localized Customer Service: Offering customer service in the local language and aligning with regional expectations can overcome skepticism.

Secure Payments and Logistics

Offering Buyer-Friendly Payment Options

International buyers expect flexible, secure, and convenient payment methods.

Multiple Payment Methods: Support credit cards, mobile wallets (like Apple Pay, Google Pay), and local payment systems.

Cryptocurrency: Some global buyers prefer paying with digital currencies like Bitcoin or Ethereum, especially in tech-forward markets.

Payment Security: Ensure strong encryption and data protection to avoid fraud and enhance buyer confidence.

Ensuring Seamless Delivery Experiences

Logistics can make or break a customer's experience.

Fast and Reliable Shipping: Work with international logistics partners that ensure fast, reliable delivery and transparency on tracking.

Customs Handling: Provide clear information about customs duties, taxes, and shipping restrictions to avoid any surprises for buyers.

Returns and Refunds: Implement a simple and clear returns process that accommodates international customers.

Chapter 24

Case Studies of Global Success

Successful Brands Reaching Billions

Lessons from Amazon, Alibaba, and Other Giants

These companies set the standard for reaching billions of buyers worldwide.

Amazon: Focus on customer-centricity, massive product offerings, and fast delivery. Amazon's vast distribution network and advanced AI-driven recommendations allow for scalability.

Alibaba: Leverages the power of its e-commerce platforms (like AliExpress) and integrates social media, payment systems (Alipay), and logistics to provide a seamless global shopping experience.

Shopify: Offers small businesses the tools to scale and sell globally, from store setup to shipping solutions.

Small Businesses Going Global

Inspiring Stories of SMEs Tapping into Global Markets

Many small businesses have successfully expanded into international markets.

Example: A local artisan jewelry brand using Instagram and Etsy to reach customers worldwide, showcasing the power of social media marketing.

Global Niche Market: How niche businesses focused on unique products, like eco-friendly goods or specialty foods, can thrive in international markets by appealing to conscious consumers.

Chapter 25

Trends Shaping the Future of Buying

The Role of AI and Automation

Chatbots, Recommendation Engines, and Beyond

AI is transforming the buying experience.

Chatbots: Automate customer service, answer FAQs, and even assist with transactions in real time.

Recommendation Engines: Personalized recommendations based on customer behavior increase sales and customer satisfaction.

Predictive Analytics: AI analyzes customer behavior patterns to predict future buying decisions, helping to tailor marketing strategies.

Sustainability and Ethical Buying

How Conscious Consumerism is Reshaping Markets

Sustainable Products: Consumers are increasingly looking for products that are eco-friendly, ethically sourced, and support social causes.

Ethical Marketing: Brands must transparently communicate their commitment to sustainability and ethical practices, which resonates with modern buyers who care about environmental and social impacts.

Chapter 26

Metrics for Measuring Success

KPIs for Global Buyer Growth

Customer Acquisition Cost, Lifetime Value, and Conversion Rates

Customer Acquisition Cost (CAC): Calculate how much it costs to acquire a customer in different regions and optimize marketing spend.

Lifetime Value (LTV): Understand how much a customer will generate over their lifetime to gauge the effectiveness of retention strategies.

Conversion Rate Optimization: Track how well your website converts visitors into buyers. Testing and refining the user experience can boost conversion rates.

Feedback Loops

Using Buyer Data to Refine Strategies

Feedback from customers is crucial to staying ahead.

Surveys and Polls: Collect feedback to identify pain points and areas for improvement.

Customer Segmentation: Use data analytics to segment customers based on behaviors, preferences, and buying habits to offer tailored experiences.

Chapter 27

Challenges and How to Overcome Them

Cultural Barriers

Overcoming Stereotypes and Biases

Understanding cultural differences is key to successful global expansion.

Local Research: Conduct thorough market research to understand local tastes, cultural norms, and potential sensitivities.

Tailored Messaging: Customize marketing campaigns to reflect local values and avoid stereotypes.

Regulatory and Legal Hurdles

Navigating International Laws and Tariffs

Compliance: Stay updated on international laws regarding product standards, taxation, and data protection (GDPR in Europe).

Customs and Duties: Be transparent with customers about potential import taxes and customs charges, ensuring a smooth purchasing experience.

Chapter 28

Action Plan to Reach One Billion Buyers

Step-by-Step Guide

From Market Research to Scaling

Market Research: Identify high-growth regions and target demographics using data and insights.

Product Development: Tailor products for different markets based on local demand and preferences.

Global Launch: Plan a phased launch to scale operations in new markets effectively.

Setting Achievable Milestones

Set clear goals and milestones for reaching different buyer segments, such as reaching 1 million, 10 million, and eventually 1 billion buyers.

Conclusion: The Billion-Buyer Blueprint

Recap of Key Strategies

Review the strategies shared throughout the book, emphasizing digital marketing, building trust, and overcoming challenges.

Encouragement to Think Big and Start Now

The goal is to inspire readers to take action, focusing on long-term growth, innovation, and global outreach to tap into the vast market of one billion buyers.

Chapter 29

$100 million dollar companies

Here are some examples of $100 million dollar companies from different industries worldwide. These companies have achieved substantial success due to their innovative business models, market leadership, or disruptive products/services:

Technology & Software

Stripe (USA) – Payment processing platform.

Zoom (USA) – Video conferencing software.

Canva (Australia) – Online design and publishing tool.

Shopify (Canada) – E-commerce platform for online stores.

UiPath (Romania/USA) – Robotic Process Automation (RPA).

E-Commerce

Mercado Libre (Argentina) – Leading e-commerce platform in Latin America.

Shein (China) – Fast fashion e-commerce retailer.

Flipkart (India) – E-commerce marketplace owned by Walmart.

Etsy (USA) – Marketplace for handmade and vintage items.

Jumia (Africa) – E-commerce platform operating in several African countries.

Consumer Goods & Services

Warby Parker (USA) – Affordable eyewear brand.

Dollar Shave Club (USA) – Subscription razor and grooming products.

Oatly (Sweden) – Oat milk and plant-based food products.

Dyson (UK) – High-tech household appliances.

Patagonia (USA) – Sustainable outdoor apparel.

Health & Wellness

Peloton (USA) – Connected fitness equipment and subscription classes.

Beyond Meat (USA) – Plant-based meat substitutes.

1mg (India) – Online pharmacy and healthcare platform.

GoodRx (USA) – Prescription discount and telehealth services.

HealthifyMe (India) – Digital health and fitness app.

FinTech

Revolut (UK) – Financial services, including banking and crypto.

Chime (USA) – Mobile banking services.

Nubank (Brazil) – Digital bank in Latin America.

Klarna (Sweden) – Buy now, pay later service.

Robinhood (USA) – Stock trading and investment app.

Media & Entertainment

Spotify (Sweden) – Music streaming platform.

Twitch (USA) – Live streaming for gaming and content creation.

Netflix (USA) – Streaming entertainment services.

Duolingo (USA) – Language learning app.

Riot Games (USA) – Video game developer, known for League of Legends.

Transportation & Mobility

Uber (USA) – Ride-hailing and delivery services.

Bolt (Estonia) – Transportation, delivery, and e-scooter rentals.

Bird (USA) – Electric scooter sharing.

Lime (USA) – Micro-mobility solutions.

Grab (Southeast Asia) – Ride-hailing and delivery services.

Real Estate & Hospitality

Airbnb (USA) – Vacation rental marketplace.

Zillow (USA) – Online real estate platform.

OYO Rooms (India) – Budget hotel network.

WeWork (USA) – Shared office spaces.

Redfin (USA) – Real estate brokerage and listing service.

Chapter 30

How these companies succeeded and how to replicate their success.

1. Solving Real Problems with Clear Value Propositions

Success Stories:

Uber simplified urban transportation by making rides accessible via a smartphone app.

Spotify solved the issue of music piracy by offering a legal, affordable, and seamless streaming experience.

How to Replicate:

Find a Pain Point: Identify a problem that a large audience faces frequently.

Deliver Value: Offer a simple, affordable, or innovative solution.

2. Leveraging Technology to Scale

Success Stories:

Stripe scaled by providing developers with simple APIs for payment processing.

Shopify created an easy-to-use platform that allowed small businesses to go online.

How to Replicate:

Automate Processes: Build scalable technology that minimizes manual intervention.

Focus on User Experience: Make your product easy to adopt and integrate.

3. Building Strong Brand Loyalty

Success Stories:

Patagonia resonated with environmentally conscious customers through sustainability efforts.

Dollar Shave Club used humor and personality to create a relatable brand.

How to Replicate:

Align with Values: Stand for something that your audience cares about.

Engage Through Storytelling: Build a community around your brand with authentic narratives.

4. Innovating Existing Markets

Success Stories:

Airbnb transformed hospitality by letting people monetize their homes.

Warby Parker disrupted the eyewear market with affordable and stylish frames sold directly online.

How to Replicate:

Identify Inefficiencies: Look for industries with outdated models or high costs.

Redefine Norms: Introduce a new way of thinking about value in that market.

5. Creating Network Effects

Success Stories:

Facebook grew because more users made the platform more valuable.

Twitch attracted both streamers and viewers, reinforcing its ecosystem.

How to Replicate:

Focus on Community: Build features that encourage users to engage and invite others.

Reward Early Adopters: Offer incentives for bringing in more users.

6. Riding Market Trends

Success Stories:

Beyond Meat capitalized on the growing demand for plant-based diets.

Zoom became essential during the COVID-19 pandemic when remote work surged.

How to Replicate:

Stay Updated: Continuously monitor market trends and consumer behavior.

Act Quickly: Be prepared to pivot or scale when demand spikes.

7. Strong Monetization Strategies

Success Stories:

Netflix moved from DVD rentals to a subscription model for streaming.

Klarna grew by charging merchants for enabling installment payments.

How to Replicate:

Prioritize Recurring Revenue: Focus on subscription-based or repeatable income streams.

Deliver ROI: Ensure that customers perceive clear benefits for what they pay.

8. Strategic Partnerships

Success Stories:

Flipkart partnered with Walmart, gaining resources and expertise.

Peloton partnered with fitness influencers and studios to enhance its reach.

How to Replicate:

Identify Synergies: Collaborate with organizations that complement your business.

Leverage Resources: Use partnerships to access new customers, markets, or technologies.

9. Scaling Globally

Success Stories:

Grab adapted Uber's model to Southeast Asia's unique needs.

Canva offered a global solution with localized content.

How to Replicate:

Start Local, Think Global: Solve local problems that can be scaled globally.

Adapt to Cultures: Tailor your product to fit different market needs.

10. Building Resilient Teams and Cultures

Success Stories:

Dyson invested heavily in R&D to stay ahead of competitors.

Chime built a team focused on simplifying personal finance for users.

How to Replicate:

Hire Visionaries: Build a team that shares your mission and innovates continuously.

Foster Innovation: Encourage experimentation and embrace failure as part of learning.

By combining these strategies with a focus on customer needs, strong execution, and a scalable business model, you can replicate the success of $100 million companies.

Chapter 31

Starting your $100 million dream business

In today's world, starting your own business has never been easier. Seriously, the barriers to entry are practically non-existent! It's no wonder that so many people are dreaming about launching a successful online venture. But here's the kicker: while tons of folks are picturing their lives filled with financial freedom and the ability to work from a beach in Bali, very few actually know how to turn that dream into a reality, especially when it comes to building a business worth, say, $100 million. And let me tell you, this isn't just another drop-shipping tale; it's a deep dive into the exciting world of global commerce, where the right moves can transform a simple click into a tidal wave of cash.

Picture this: you wake up to your phone buzzing with notifications, cha-ching! Sales are rolling in while you're just sipping your morning coffee. That's the magic of dropshipping. You don't have to deal with the hassle of stocking products or managing inventory. Nope! You're like a middleman, connecting suppliers with customers, all while taking advantage of the internet to build a thriving business from the cozy corner of your home. All you really need is a laptop and a decent internet connection, and suddenly, the whole world is your marketplace. You can reach customers from every nook and cranny of the globe!

But, hold on, where do you even start? The first step is all about finding your niche. In a marketplace that's overflowing with options, you've gotta stand out. Whether you're super passionate about eco-friendly products or can't get enough of the latest tech gadgets, nailing down a specific niche can help you attract a loyal audience that's eager to connect with your brand. This book is your trusty guide, walking you through how to research trends and what customers are into, helping you carve out your own little corner in the market.

Once you've figured out your niche, the next big challenge is sourcing your products. This is where your dropshipping success really hinges on finding reliable suppliers who can deliver quality goods to your customers. With platforms like AliExpress and Oberlo at your fingertips, the options are endless. But, and this is a big but, you've gotta prioritize quality control. Ordering samples before diving in with a supplier can save you from a world of hurt later on.

Now, building your online store is where the fun really begins. It's a mix of creativity and strategy. Thanks to user-friendly platforms like Shopify and WooCommerce, you can whip up a stunning storefront that not only showcases your products but also tells your brand's story. Your website should feel like a warm welcome mat for your audience, making it super easy for them to navigate and discover what you've got to offer. Trust me, compelling product descriptions and high-quality images are your best friends in this endeavor.

But here's the thing, even the prettiest store won't sell itself. Marketing is the lifeblood of your business. Social media platforms like Instagram and Facebook are fantastic stages for promoting your products, and teaming up with influencers can help you reach a much wider audience. Don't sleep on email marketing, either! It's often underestimated but can keep your customers engaged and in the loop, turning one-time buyers into loyal fans.

As your business starts to grow, you'll quickly realize the power of automation. Imagine being able to free yourself from the nitty-gritty tasks like inventory management and order processing. With the right tools, you can streamline your operations, giving you more time to focus on what really matters, growing your brand and expanding your reach.

Understanding global markets is key in our interconnected world. Every country has its own unique buying habits and preferences, and tapping into these nuances can give you a serious edge. With a bit of research, you can tweak your strategies to cater to different audiences, making international sales not just a pipe dream, but a real possibility.

And let's not forget about customer service, it's the backbone of any successful business. Providing quick and effective support can turn a one-time buyer into a repeat customer. By addressing inquiries promptly and resolving issues efficiently, you're building trust and loyalty. Consider adding Chatbots to your customer service toolkit to ensure help is available 24/7.

Now, let's talk about data, your most valuable asset. Keeping an eye on sales trends and website traffic can provide you with insights that drive your growth. Tools like Google Analytics are absolute gold when it comes to understanding customer behavior, enabling you to refine your approach and boost your bottom line.

Scaling your business is the ultimate goal, and this book is packed with the knowledge you need to expand your product range and explore new markets. As your workload increases, hiring virtual assistants can lighten the load, allowing you to keep your focus on innovation and customer satisfaction.

Branding is more than just a logo; it's the soul of your business. A strong brand identity resonates with customers on an emotional level, creating lasting impressions. Consistency is key, make sure your website, social media, and packaging all reflect your brand's message and values.

Managing finances can feel overwhelming, but it's absolutely essential for keeping your business afloat. You'll need to keep tabs on income and expenses, understand taxes, and navigate regulations in different countries, all part of the entrepreneurial journey. With the right tools, you can simplify this process and ensure your business stays healthy and compliant.

Let's be real, challenges are going to pop up. But you know what? They're also opportunities for growth. Whether it's dealing with supplier delays or handling customer complaints, learning to navigate these bumps in the road will make you a more resilient entrepreneur. Embrace those setbacks; they're just stepping stones on your path to success.

As the e-commerce landscape continues to evolve, staying ahead of trends is crucial. The future of dropshipping is looking bright, with new technologies and shifting consumer expectations shaping the market. Sustainability and ethical sourcing are becoming increasingly important, and adapting to these trends will set your business up for long-term success.

So, here's the deal: this book is your roadmap to mastering the art of dropshipping and building a business that not only thrives but also resonates with customers around the globe. Dive in, embrace the journey, and get ready to unlock the incredible potential of global markets. Your entrepreneurial adventure starts now!

Chapter 32

Understanding Dropshipping

Let's kick things off with a little chat about dropshipping. You know, that buzzword that's been flying around the internet like a squirrel on caffeine? Well, here's the deal: dropshipping is a business model where you sell products without ever having to keep them in stock. Yeah, you heard me right. You don't need a warehouse full of gadgets, gizmos, or even that funky lava lamp you bought on a whim.

Picture this: You're lounging on your couch, scrolling through your phone, and BAM! Someone buys a pair of those trendy sneakers you've been promoting. Instead of rushing to your garage to dig through boxes, you simply contact your supplier, place the order, and let them handle the shipping. Easy, right?

Now, let's dig deeper into why this model is such a game changer. First off, it slashes your financial risk. You only buy the product from a supplier AFTER you make a sale. That's right! No more pouring your hard-earned cash into inventory that might just collect dust. You can start a business without breaking the bank. And trust me, as someone who's made more than a few financial blunders in the past, I can tell you that this is a blessing.

Think about it: you can run this whole operation from anywhere in the world. All you need is a computer and an internet connection. I once set up a dropshipping store while sipping a piña colada on a beach in Mexico. Okay, maybe that's a slight exaggeration, but you get the picture. You can be sitting in your pajamas at home or sipping coffee at your favorite café. The world is your oyster, my friend.

So, let's break it down further. Here are three main points to help you understand dropshipping like a pro:

1. No Inventory, No Problem: With dropshipping, you're not tied down by inventory. This means you can offer a wide range of products without the hassle of managing stock. Want to sell quirky kitchen gadgets, trendy apparel, or even the latest tech? Go for it! You can pivot your product offerings based on what's hot or what's not. It's like being a chameleon in the business world.

2. Financial Freedom: The beauty of this model is that it minimizes your financial risk. You're not investing in products until you've made a sale. This means you can test out different niches without shelling out a ton of cash. Plus, if a product doesn't sell, you're not stuck with a mountain of unsold inventory. It's a win-win!

3. Global Reach: Imagine being able to sell to customers around the globe with just a few clicks. That's the magic of dropshipping. You can tap into international markets without ever leaving your living room. Want to sell to customers in Europe, Asia, or even Antarctica? Okay, maybe not Antarctica, but you get the idea. The world is your playground, and you can access it all with the right online strategies.

Now, let's dive a bit deeper into each of these points because understanding dropshipping is like peeling an onion—there are layers, and sometimes it might make you cry, but it's totally worth it.

First up, let's chat about inventory. One of the biggest headaches in traditional retail is managing stock. You have to worry about what to order, how much to order, and where to store it. It's like trying to solve a Rubik's Cube while riding a unicycle. With dropshipping, you can skip all that drama. You can list as many products as you want on your site, and if someone buys it, you simply reach out to your supplier. They handle the fulfillment, and you sit back and enjoy the profits.

This flexibility allows you to experiment with different products and niches. You can test the waters without diving in headfirst. Say you're curious about selling eco-friendly products. You can start by listing a few items and see how they perform. If they take off, great! If not, no harm done. You just switch gears and try something else.

Now, let's talk money—specifically, how dropshipping can help you keep more of it in your pocket. In traditional retail, you're often stuck with upfront costs for inventory. You might invest thousands of dollars in products that could flop. But with dropshipping, you only pay for what you sell. This means you can focus on marketing and growing your brand instead of worrying about what's gathering dust in your garage.

And here's a little secret: you can start dropshipping with a few hundred bucks. That's right! You don't need a fortune to get started. Just a solid idea, some hustle, and a reliable supplier. As you grow, you can reinvest your profits into your business, scaling up as you go.

Finally, let's touch on the global reach. With dropshipping, you're not limited to your local market. You can sell to anyone, anywhere, as long as you have an internet connection. This opens up a world of opportunities. You can tap into emerging markets or niche communities that traditional retailers might overlook.

Think about it: if you're selling a unique product that resonates with a specific audience, you can find customers in places you never imagined. You could be selling handmade jewelry to someone in Australia while sipping coffee in your hometown diner. It's a beautiful thing, isn't it?

But wait, there's more! The beauty of dropshipping is that it allows you to be agile. Trends come and go faster than you can say "viral TikTok." With dropshipping, you can pivot your product offerings based on what's trending. If a new gadget hits the market and everyone's buzzing about it, you can quickly add it to your store without worrying about stock.

Now, I know what you're thinking. "This sounds great, but what about competition?" Well, let me tell you, competition is a part of any business. But here's the kicker: with dropshipping, you can differentiate yourself through branding, customer service, and unique marketing strategies.

You don't have to be the cheapest option on the block. Instead, focus on building a brand that resonates with your audience. Share your story, engage with your customers, and create a community around your products. When people connect with your brand, they're more likely to choose you over the competition, even if your prices are a bit higher.

So, here's a quick recap of what we've covered:

- Dropshipping allows you to sell products without holding inventory.
- You only pay for products after making a sale, minimizing financial risk.
- You can reach customers around the world with just a computer and internet connection.

Now, before we wrap this up, let's talk about some practical steps you can take to get started with dropshipping.

1. Choose Your Niche: Think about what you're passionate about or what interests you. Do some research to see what's trending.

2. Find Reliable Suppliers: Look for suppliers with good reviews and a solid track record. Websites like AliExpress, Oberlo, or even local wholesalers can be great places to start.

3. Set Up Your Online Store: Use platforms like Shopify or WooCommerce to create your store. Make it visually appealing and easy to navigate.

4. Market Your Products: Utilize social media, email marketing, and SEO to drive traffic to your store. Don't be afraid to get creative with your marketing strategies!

5. Analyze and Optimize: Keep track of your sales and customer feedback. Use this data to refine your product offerings and marketing tactics.

So, there you have it! Dropshipping is a fantastic way to enter the world of e-commerce with minimal risk and maximum flexibility. You can build a thriving business that allows you to work from anywhere and tap into global markets. Just remember, it's not just about selling products; it's about creating a brand that resonates with your audience.

Now, go out there and start your dropshipping journey! You've got this!

To truly understand dropshipping, let's explore some more nuanced aspects. After all, the devil is in the details, and the details can make or break your business.

One of the most important elements of dropshipping is choosing the right products. Think of it as curating a playlist. You want a mix of crowd-pleasers and hidden gems. Start by researching trends on platforms like Google Trends, social media, and even Amazon's best-seller lists. What are people raving about? What's gaining traction?

Next, let's talk about supplier relationships. Your supplier is your lifeline in the dropshipping world. A good supplier can make your life easier, while a bad one can send you spiraling into chaos. Look for suppliers who are responsive, have a good reputation, and offer quality products. Test their service before fully committing. Place a small order and see how they handle it. If they deliver on time and the product meets your standards, you might have found a keeper.

Once you've got your niche and suppliers sorted, it's time to build your online presence. Your website is your storefront, and first impressions matter. Make it user-friendly, visually appealing, and optimized for mobile devices. People shop on their phones more than ever, so ensure your site is responsive. Use high-quality images, compelling product descriptions, and customer reviews to build trust.

Now, let's get into marketing. You can have the best products in the world, but if no one knows about them, you're just shouting into the void. Utilize social media platforms like Instagram, Facebook, and TikTok to showcase your products. Create engaging content that resonates with your audience. Consider using influencers to reach a broader audience. Just make sure their values align with your brand.

Email marketing is another powerful tool. Build an email list from day one. Offer incentives for sign-ups, like discounts or exclusive content. Regularly send out newsletters featuring new products, promotions, and valuable content related to your niche. This keeps your audience engaged and coming back for more.

As you grow, don't forget to track your metrics. Use analytics tools to monitor your website traffic, conversion rates, and customer behavior. This data is gold. It tells you what's working and what needs tweaking.

Finally, let's talk about scaling your business. Once you've got a solid foundation, it's time to think bigger. Consider expanding your product line, exploring new markets, or even creating your own branded products. The beauty of dropshipping is that it allows you to scale without the headaches of traditional retail.

In conclusion, dropshipping is not just a business model; it's a lifestyle choice. It offers flexibility, financial freedom, and the ability to reach a global audience. By understanding the ins and outs of this model, you can build a successful business that not only meets your financial goals but also aligns with your passions.

So, what are you waiting for? The world of dropshipping is waiting for you to dive in. Embrace the adventure, learn as you go, and don't be afraid to make mistakes. Each misstep is a lesson that will bring you one step closer to success. Now go out there and start building your $100 million dropshipping empire! You've got this!

Chapter 33

Finding Your Niche: A Journey worth Taking

Alright, folks! Let's jump right into the world of niches. So, what's a niche, you might be wondering? Picture it like this: it's that elusive perfect pair of jeans—one that fits just right and makes you feel like a million bucks. You know, the kind you can wear anywhere and feel totally confident? Well, that's what a niche is all about. It's a specific market segment where you can really shine. Maybe you're into eco-friendly products, or perhaps tech gadgets are your jam. Maybe you've got a soft spot for quirky cat toys (who doesn't love a good cat toy?). The key here is to focus on something that gets your heart racing. Because let's be real—if you're not excited about it, how can you expect anyone else to be?

Now, here's the deal. Choosing a niche isn't just about what you personally like; it's a savvy business move, too. When you pick a niche, you stand out like a sore thumb in a sea of sameness. Think about it: you're at a party, and someone starts raving about their obsession with vintage vinyl records. Wouldn't you want to chime in and share your thoughts? That's the kind of vibe you want to create with your niche. You want to attract people who share your passion and are eager to buy what you're selling.

So, how do you find this golden niche? Well, it all starts with a bit of research. I know, I know—research sounds about as exciting as watching paint dry. But hang tight! Researching trends and customer interests is like being a detective in your own little market. You've got to dig deep and figure out what people really want. You can use tools like Google Trends, social media hashtags, and even good old-fashioned surveys. Seriously, don't hesitate to ask your friends and family what they're into. You'd be amazed at the gems you might uncover.

Let me share a little story from my own journey. When I first started out, I thought I'd dive headfirst into the world of fitness products. I mean, who doesn't want to get fit, right? But after a few months of floundering around, I realized that my heart just wasn't in it. I was, well, kinda just another fish in a big ol' ocean of fitness gurus. So, I pivoted. I began exploring sustainable products—eco-friendly stuff that actually made a difference. And guess what? My sales skyrocketed! I was finally speaking to a passionate audience, and it felt fantastic.

Now, let's break this down into some actionable steps, shall we? Here's how to find your niche like a pro:

1. Identify Your Interests: What are you passionate about? What gets you fired up? Make a list of your hobbies, interests, and anything that makes you want to jump out of bed in the morning.

2. Research Trends: Use tools like Google Trends or BuzzSumo to see what's hot. Look for rising trends in your areas of interest. Are people searching for eco-friendly home goods? Are tech gadgets on the rise?

3. Analyze the Competition: Check out what others are doing in your potential niche. Are they successful? What gaps can you fill? This is super important. You want to find a niche that's not already overcrowded.

4. Test the Waters: Before you dive in headfirst, consider testing your niche with a small product launch. Platforms like Etsy or eBay can help you gauge interest. If you get a positive response, you're onto something!

5. Stay Flexible: The market is always changing. Don't be afraid to pivot if something isn't working. Remember, you're the captain of this ship.

Now, let's talk about why picking a niche is so important. Imagine you're at a buffet. You've got a little bit of everything on your plate, but it all looks like a mishmash of flavors. Not appealing, right? That's what a non-niche business looks like. But if you focus on a specific area, you create a cohesive brand that people can connect with. You become the go-to expert in your field. And trust me, customers love that.

When you focus on a niche, you're not just selling products; you're building a community. You're creating a space where people feel understood and valued. It's like hosting a dinner party where everyone shares the same interests. That's the kind of atmosphere you want to cultivate.

Now, let's dig into the nitty-gritty of researching trends and customer interests. This is where the magic happens! Here's a handy list of tools and methods to help you get started:

- Google Trends: This is your best friend. Type in keywords related to your interests and see how they've trended over time. You can even compare different terms to see which one is gaining traction.

- Social Media: Platforms like Instagram and Pinterest are gold mines for spotting trends. Look at what influencers are promoting. Check out popular hashtags related to your niche.

- Online Forums: Dive into Reddit or niche-specific forums. See what people are discussing. What problems are they facing? What solutions are they seeking?

- Surveys: Don't underestimate the power of a simple survey. Use tools like Survey-Monkey or Google Forms to ask potential customers about their interests. You'll gain invaluable insights!

- Competitor Analysis: Keep an eye on your competitors. What are they doing well? Where are they lacking? This can give you clues about what customers are looking for.

Remember, folks, finding your niche isn't a one-and-done deal. It's an ongoing process. You've got to stay curious and open-minded.

Trends change faster than you can say "dropshipping," so keep your finger on the pulse.

In conclusion, finding your niche is all about discovering that sweet spot where your passions meet market demand. It's about standing out, attracting the right customers, and creating a community that shares your vision. So, roll up your sleeves, do your research, and get ready to carve out your space in the dropshipping world.

And hey, if you hit a bump in the road, don't sweat it. Every entrepreneur faces challenges. Just remember, the journey is just as important as the destination. So, keep pushing forward, stay adaptable, and let your niche shine!

Let's dive deeper into some of these steps, because, honestly, finding your niche is a journey, not a race. It's like a long road trip where you get to explore all sorts of interesting sights along the way. So, buckle up, and let's hit the road!

Step 1: Identify Your Interests

So, let's talk about interests. This is where the magic begins! Grab a pen and paper, or your favorite note-taking app, and jot down everything you love. Think about the things you could talk about for hours without getting bored. Is it gardening? Cooking? Maybe it's DIY crafts or even something as niche as underwater basket weaving (hey, no judgment here!).

When you're brainstorming, don't hold back. Write down everything that comes to mind, even if it seems a little out there. You never know what might spark an idea!

And here's a little tip: think about the moments when you feel most alive. What are you doing when you're happiest? Those moments can lead you straight to your niche.

Step 2: Research Trends

Okay, so you've got your list of interests. Now, it's time to do some sleuthing! Researching trends might sound like a chore, but trust me, it can be pretty enlightening.

Start with Google Trends. Type in a few keywords from your list and see how they've trended over time. Are people searching for them more now than they were a few years ago? That's a good sign!

Next, hop onto social media. Platforms like Instagram and Pinterest are buzzing with trends. You can get a real sense of what people are into right now. Follow influencers in your areas of interest and see what they're promoting.

And don't forget about online forums! Places like Reddit can be treasure troves of information. Join discussions and see what problems people are facing. This can give you insight into what solutions you could provide.

Step 3: Analyze the Competition

Now that you've got a clearer picture of what's trending, it's time to see who else is out there. Checking out the competition is like peeking into the neighbor's yard to see what they're planting.

Look at what others are doing in your potential niche. Are they successful? What are they offering? And most importantly, what gaps can you fill? This is crucial. You want to find a niche that's not already oversaturated.

Take notes on what works and what doesn't. Maybe there's a product that's getting a lot of buzz, but the reviews are lackluster. That's your opportunity to swoop in and offer something better!

Step 4: Test the Waters

Alright, you've done your homework, and you're feeling good about your niche. But before you dive in headfirst, it's smart to test the waters.

Consider launching a small product to see how it performs. Platforms like Etsy or eBay are great for this. You can gauge interest without committing a ton of resources. If people are excited about what you're offering, that's a huge green light to go full steam ahead!

And don't be afraid to ask for feedback. Reach out to your friends, family, or even social media followers. Their insights can be invaluable as you refine your offerings.

Step 5: Stay Flexible

Finally, let's talk about flexibility. The market is always changing, and that's just the nature of the beast. Don't be afraid to pivot if something isn't working.

Think of it like driving a car. Sometimes you hit a roadblock, and you've got to take a detour. That's okay! The important thing is to keep moving forward.

You're the captain of this ship, and you've got the power to steer it in a new direction if you need to. Just stay curious and open-minded, and you'll find your way.

Now, let's circle back to why all of this matters. Finding your niche isn't just about selling products; it's about creating a community. When you focus on a specific area, you're not just another faceless business. You become a trusted resource for people who share your interests.

Imagine hosting a dinner party where everyone is talking about the same thing. It's a warm, inviting atmosphere where everyone feels understood. That's the kind of vibe you want to create with your niche.

And here's the kicker: when you build a community, you're not just attracting customers; you're attracting loyal fans. These are the people who will rave about your products to their friends and family. They'll become your biggest advocates, and that's worth its weight in gold.

So, as you embark on this journey to find your niche, remember to stay true to yourself. Embrace your passions, do your research, and don't be afraid to take risks.

And if you ever hit a bump in the road, just know you're not alone. Every entrepreneur faces challenges, and it's all part of the process. The journey is just as important as the destination, so keep pushing forward.

In the end, finding your niche is about discovering that sweet spot where your passions meet market demand. It's about standing out, attracting the right customers, and creating a community that shares your vision.

So, roll up those sleeves, dive into your research, and get ready to carve out your space in the world. You've got this! And remember, the adventure is just beginning.

Chapter 34

Finding the right suppliers

Finding the right suppliers for your dropshipping business can feel like searching for a needle in a haystack—except that needle is actually a golden ticket to your success. Trust me, you want to partner with suppliers who deliver quality products on time and keep your customers smiling. So, how do you go about finding these elusive gems? Let's dive in and break it down together.

First things first, you need to know where to start your search. Websites like AliExpress and Oberlo are basically the Amazon of the dropshipping universe. They connect you with manufacturers and suppliers from all corners of the globe. Seriously, it's like having a massive marketplace right at your fingertips. You can scroll through thousands of products with just a few clicks. But, hang on a sec! Not all suppliers are created equal, and that's where things can get a bit tricky.

Here's the thing: You can't just jump in and start selling without doing your homework. I mean, you wouldn't buy a car without taking it for a test drive, right? Well, the same principle applies to dropshipping. Always, and I mean always, order samples before you commit to a supplier. This step is absolutely crucial. You want to check the quality of the product and make sure it matches the description. There's nothing worse than selling a product that doesn't live up to expectations. Trust me, I learned this the hard way when I sold a batch of phone cases that were flimsier than a wet paper towel. It was a total disaster.

Now, let's chat about how to evaluate your suppliers. Here are some key factors you should definitely keep in mind:

1. Product Quality: This is non-negotiable. Order samples and check everything—materials, durability, and overall quality. If it doesn't meet your standards, it's time to move on. No second chances here!

2. Shipping Times: Look for suppliers who can get your products to your customers in a reasonable time frame. If your customers are waiting weeks for their orders, they're gonna be more likely to hit that "unsubscribe" button faster than you can say "dropshipping."

3. Communication: Don't be shy! Reach out to suppliers with questions. Are they responsive? Do they provide clear answers?

Good communication is a solid sign of a reliable partner. If they're ghosting you, that's a red flag.

4.   Reviews and Ratings: This is like your supplier's report card. Check feedback from other dropshippers. If a supplier has a ton of negative reviews, steer clear. It's like dating; you want someone with a good track record!

5.   Return Policies: This is super important. Understand the return process. If a customer receives a defective product, you need to know how to handle it without losing your shirt. A good return policy can save you a lot of headaches down the road.

I know, I know—finding reliable suppliers can feel like a daunting task, but don't let that discourage you. Think of it as building a relationship. Just like in life, the right connections can make all the difference in your business.

Now, let's get a bit more personal here. When I first dipped my toes into the dropshipping pool, I was so eager to make sales that I didn't take the time to properly vet my suppliers. I was like a kid in a candy store, grabbing whatever looked shiny and promising. Spoiler alert: that strategy didn't pan out so well. I ended up with a bunch of returns and a whole lot of angry customers. It was a wake-up call, let me tell ya!

After that experience, I decided to take sourcing seriously. I created a checklist, ordered samples, and even made a spreadsheet to track my findings. Yes, I went full-on nerd mode, but it totally paid off. My sales skyrocketed once I partnered with reliable suppliers. So, take it from me: Don't skip this step. It's worth the effort.

Now, here's a little tip for you. When you're browsing on AliExpress or Oberlo, use the filters to narrow down your search. You can filter by ratings, order volume, and shipping times. This will save you a ton of time and help you find quality suppliers faster. Seriously, don't overlook this feature!

In summary, sourcing products is a vital part of your dropshipping journey. It's not just about finding a supplier; it's about finding the right supplier. So, roll up your sleeves, do your research, and don't be afraid to reach out and ask questions.

Here's a quick recap of actionable steps you can take right now:

Explore Websites: Check out AliExpress and Oberlo. Make a list of potential suppliers that catch your eye.

Order Samples: Get your hands on those products! It's quality check time, baby.

Evaluate: Use the checklist to assess each supplier based on quality, shipping, communication, reviews, and return policies.

Build Relationships: Don't just be a faceless buyer. Communicate with your suppliers and establish a rapport. A little friendliness goes a long way!

Finding the right suppliers may take some time, but it's the foundation of a successful dropshipping business. So, get out there and start sourcing like a pro!

Remember, every great business starts with a solid foundation. And that foundation? It's built on quality products and reliable suppliers. So, let's make sure you're set up for success!

Now, let's dive a bit deeper into the nitty-gritty of sourcing products. One thing I've learned over the years is that the process doesn't just stop at finding suppliers. It's an ongoing journey. You've got to keep your finger on the pulse of your suppliers and their products. The market changes, trends shift, and new suppliers pop up all the time.

Take, for example, the rise of eco-friendly products. Customers today are more conscious about sustainability than ever before. If you're not sourcing from suppliers who offer eco-friendly options, you might be missing out on a huge market. So, keep your eyes peeled for new trends and adapt accordingly.

Another thing to consider is building a brand around your products. It's not just about selling items; it's about creating a memorable experience for your customers. Think about how you can differentiate yourself from the competition. Maybe it's through unique packaging, personalized customer service, or even a killer social media presence. Whatever it is, make sure it resonates with your target audience.

Let's not forget about the importance of testing your products regularly. Just because a supplier was great last month doesn't mean they'll be great this month. Keep ordering samples periodically to ensure that the quality remains consistent. It's a bit of work, but it's so worth it to keep your customers happy and coming back for more.

And speaking of customers, let's chat about feedback. Encourage your customers to leave reviews and share their experiences with your products. This not only helps you improve but also builds trust with potential buyers. If they see that others are happy with their purchases, they're more likely to hit that "buy" button.

Now, let's take a moment to talk about pricing. Finding a supplier with great products is one thing, but you also need to make sure you're getting a good deal. Do some research to see what similar products are selling for. This will help you set competitive prices while still making a profit. Just remember, if you're charging too little, you might be undervaluing your products, and if you're charging too much, you might scare away potential customers.

Networking is another crucial aspect of sourcing. Don't be afraid to connect with other dropshippers and share experiences. Join online communities, forums, or social media groups where you can exchange tips and tricks. You'll be surprised at how much you can learn from others who've been in your shoes.

Finally, let's talk about the emotional side of sourcing. It can be frustrating at times—like when you think you've found the perfect supplier, only to discover they're unreliable or their products don't meet your standards. It's okay to feel overwhelmed. Just remember, every setback is an opportunity to learn and grow. Don't get discouraged. Keep pushing forward, and you'll find the right suppliers who will help you build a thriving dropshipping business.

In the end, sourcing products is more than just a task on your to-do list; it's a journey that can lead to incredible opportunities. So, take your time, do your research, and don't forget to enjoy the process. Building a successful dropshipping business is a marathon, not a sprint.

So, let's recap everything we've covered so far:

- Start by exploring platforms like AliExpress and Oberlo to find potential suppliers.
- Always order samples to ensure product quality.
- Evaluate suppliers based on shipping times, communication, reviews, and return policies.
- Build relationships with your suppliers for a more personal touch.

- Stay updated on market trends and adapt your sourcing strategy accordingly.
- Regularly test your products to maintain quality.
- Encourage customer feedback to improve and build trust.
- Be mindful of your pricing strategy to remain competitive.
- Network with other dropshippers to learn from their experiences.
- And most importantly, stay positive and keep pushing through the challenges.

By following these steps, you'll be well on your way to finding the right suppliers and setting the stage for a successful dropshipping business. So, roll up those sleeves, dive into the world of sourcing, and get ready to make your mark in the dropshipping arena. You've got this!

Chapter 35

Building Your Online Store

Alright, everyone, let's jump right into the world of building your online store. Seriously, this is where the magic really starts. You've got dreams of turning that little idea of yours into a thriving business—maybe even a $100 million empire. But I get it; you're probably sitting there thinking, "Okay, but where on earth do I even begin?" Don't sweat it. I'm here to help you figure it all out.

First things first, you've gotta pick a platform. Think of it like choosing the right tool for a job—like, you wouldn't use a hammer to screw in a lightbulb, right? Platforms like Shopify and WooCommerce are great options because they make it super easy to set up an online store. Seriously, they're so user-friendly that even someone who struggles with the TV remote can figure it out. You can have a professional-looking site up and running in no time, and trust me, if I can do it, so can you.

Now, let's talk about the look of your store. You want it to be visually appealing and easy to navigate. Picture your favorite diner—if the menu's a total mess, you're not sticking around, right?

Customers are the same way; they want a smooth experience. So, keep things clean and simple. Use a layout that guides them through your offerings like a friendly tour guide, not like a lost puppy trying to find its way home.

Next, let's get into the nitty-gritty—product descriptions and images. You want to make sure your product descriptions are crystal clear. Think about it: imagine walking into a store, spotting a shirt, but having no clue what size it is or what material it's made from. Frustrating, right? You don't want your customers feeling that way. Be specific! Tell them exactly what they're getting.

And let's not overlook those high-quality images. If your product photos look like they were taken with a potato, you might as well be selling air. Seriously, invest in a decent camera or hire a photographer if you can swing it. Your products deserve to shine, and so do you. Show them off like you're the proud parent at a school play, ready to brag about your kid's big moment.

Here's a little tip: when you're writing those descriptions, keep your audience in mind. What are they looking for? What problems are they trying to solve? Address those needs head-on. Use language that resonates with them. You're not just selling a product; you're offering a solution to their problems.

Alright, let's break it down into some actionable steps, shall we?

1. Choose Your Platform: Decide between Shopify, WooCommerce, or another platform that fits your needs. Don't overthink it; just pick one and dive in.

2. Design Your Store: Focus on clean, easy navigation. Use colors and fonts that reflect your brand. Remember, first impressions matter!

3. Write Clear Descriptions: Be specific. Include size, color, material, and benefits. What makes your product stand out?

4. Use Quality Images: Invest in good photography. Show your product from multiple angles and in action.

5. Test Your Store: Before you launch, have friends or family navigate your site. Get feedback and make adjustments.

You might be wondering, "How long will this take?" Well, if you dedicate a solid weekend, you could have a functioning store up and running. But remember, this is just the beginning. Building a successful online store is like planting a garden. You've got to nurture it, water it, and give it some sunshine to see it grow.

As you're setting up your store, keep an eye on trends. What's hot right now? What are people buzzing about? Staying in the loop will help you tailor your offerings to what customers want. It's like being a DJ at a party—you've got to know which songs will keep the dance floor packed.

Speaking of trends, let's chat about some common misconceptions. Some folks think that once they launch their store, the sales will just roll in. Spoiler alert: that's not how it works. You've got to market your store, engage with your audience, and build relationships. Think of it like dating—nobody wants to commit after a first date, right? You've got to woo them a little.

Now, let's pivot for a second. I remember when I first launched my store. I was so pumped; I thought I'd wake up to a flood of orders. But reality hit hard. I quickly realized I needed to hustle. I started promoting my products on social media, reaching out to influencers, and even running ads. It took time, but eventually, the sales started to trickle in. And that's when I knew I was onto something.

So, don't get discouraged if you don't see immediate results. Keep pushing, keep refining your approach, and most importantly, keep learning.

As you embark on this journey, surround yourself with resources. There are tons of online courses, forums, and communities filled with people just like you—ready to share their experiences and tips. Leverage those resources. You don't have to go it alone.

And hey, don't forget to celebrate the small wins. Did you get your first sale? Do a little happy dance! Did someone leave a positive review? Treat yourself to a slice of cake! These little victories will keep you motivated on the road ahead.

Now, let's wrap this up with some final thoughts. Building your online store is an exciting adventure. It's a chance to create something that reflects your passion and vision. But remember, it takes effort, persistence, and a sprinkle of creativity.

So, roll up your sleeves, get to work, and let's make this happen. You've got this! Your future customers are out there, just waiting to discover what you have to offer. Now go out there and build that store like the rockstar entrepreneur you are!

Okay, so now that we've covered the basics, let's dive deeper into some of the more intricate parts of running an online store. It's not just about setting it up and hoping for the best. No way! You've gotta be proactive, keep learning, and adapt as you go. So, let's break it down further.

Once you've got your store up and running, it's time to focus on marketing. This is where you really get to show off your products and connect with your audience. Social media is your best friend here. Platforms like Instagram, Facebook, and Pinterest can help you reach potential customers in a way that feels personal and engaging.

Start by creating a content calendar. Trust me, this will save you a ton of stress later on. Plan out what you want to post, when you want to post it, and what your goals are for each piece of content. Are you showcasing a new product? Running a sale? Sharing customer testimonials? Having a plan will keep you organized and help you stay consistent.

And speaking of consistency, that's key. You want to create a recognizable brand presence online. Use the same colors, fonts, and tone of voice across all your platforms. This way, when people see your posts, they'll instantly know it's you. It's like a signature style; it makes you memorable.

Now, let's talk about engagement. Don't just post and ghost! Take the time to respond to comments, answer questions, and interact with your followers. This builds a sense of community around your brand. People love to feel connected, and if they see that you're genuinely interested in what they have to say, they're more likely to become loyal customers.

Another effective marketing strategy is email marketing. I know, I know, it sounds a bit old-school, but trust me, it works. Start building an email list from day one. Offer something valuable in exchange for email sign-ups—maybe a discount on their first purchase or a free e-book related to your niche. Once you have a list, you can send out newsletters, promotions, and updates. Just remember to keep it engaging and not too salesy. People appreciate value, not just constant pitches.

And let's not forget about SEO—search engine optimization. It sounds a bit technical, but it's really just about making sure your store shows up in search results. Use relevant keywords in your product descriptions, blog posts, and even your store's meta descriptions. This helps search engines understand what your store is about, making it easier for potential customers to find you.

Now, if you're feeling a bit overwhelmed, that's totally normal. Running an online store is a lot of work, and it's easy to get lost in the details. So, here's a little secret: take it one step at a time. Focus on one area of your business each week. Maybe this week you'll work on your social media strategy, and next week you'll tackle your email marketing. Breaking it down makes it feel more manageable.

And hey, don't forget to analyze your results. Use tools like Google Analytics to track your website traffic and see where your customers are coming from. This data is gold! It'll help you understand what's working and what needs tweaking. If you notice that a particular product is flying off the shelves, double down on promoting that. If something's not performing well, don't be afraid to pivot and try something new.

As you grow, you might want to consider expanding your product line. This is where you can really get creative! Think about what else your customers might want or need. You could add complementary products, or even branch out into a new category entirely. Just make sure it aligns with your brand and what your audience is looking for.

And let's not forget about customer service. This is crucial. You want to make sure your customers feel valued and heard. Respond to inquiries promptly, resolve issues efficiently, and always be polite. Happy customers are more likely to return and recommend your store to others. Plus, word of mouth is a powerful marketing tool.

Now, let's take a moment to talk about the emotional side of this journey. Building an online store can be a rollercoaster ride—there are highs, lows, and everything in between. You might feel excited one minute and completely overwhelmed the next. That's okay! It's all part of the process. Just remember to be kind to yourself. Celebrate your victories, no matter how small, and don't dwell too much on the setbacks. They're just stepping stones on your path to success.

As you continue on this journey, remember that you're not alone. There's a whole community of entrepreneurs out there, and many of them have been where you are now. Seek out forums, Facebook groups, or even local meetups where you can connect with others in the same boat. Sharing experiences, tips, and advice can be incredibly valuable.

And don't forget to keep learning! The online business landscape is always changing, so it's important to stay up-to-date with the latest trends and best practices. There are tons of resources available—blogs, podcasts, online courses—so take advantage of them. The more you know, the better equipped you'll be to tackle whatever comes your way.

Finally, let's wrap things up with a little pep talk. Building your online store is an exciting adventure, but it's also a lot of work. It's a chance to create something that reflects your passion and vision. Just remember, it takes effort, persistence, and a sprinkle of creativity.

So, roll up those sleeves, get to work, and let's make this happen. You've got this! Your future customers are out there, just waiting to discover what you have to offer. Now go out there and build that store like the rockstar entrepreneur you are!

And remember, every big journey starts with a single step. So take that step today, and keep moving forward. You're on the right path, and I can't wait to see where it takes you!

Chapter 36

Marketing Strategies

Alright, folks, let's dive into the world of marketing strategies! Now, if you think marketing is just about throwing money at ads and hoping for the best, let me tell ya, you're in for a wild ride. We're talking about smart, savvy ways to promote your dropshipping business that'll have your sales soaring faster than a Midwest tornado!

First off, let's chat about social media. I mean, come on, who isn't scrolling through Instagram or Facebook these days? It's like the digital town square, where everyone gathers to see what's hot and what's not. So, if you're not promoting your products on these platforms, you're missing out big time.

Imagine this: you've got a killer product, but nobody knows about it. That's like having a pizza shop in a ghost town—no customers, no sales. Use Instagram and Facebook to showcase your products. Post eye-catching images, create engaging stories, and run ads that pop. People love visuals! And trust me, a well-placed Instagram story can lead to a flood of traffic to your store.

Now, let's talk about influencer marketing. This is like the secret sauce of social media. You find someone with a following that aligns with your target market and BOOM! You've got a fast track to a larger audience. Think of influencers as the cool kids in high school; if they're wearing it, everyone wants it.

But how do you find the right influencer? Start by looking for folks who are already talking about products similar to yours. You want someone who genuinely believes in what they're promoting, not just cashing a check. Reach out, offer them your product, and let them share their thoughts. You'll be amazed at how quickly their followers will want to check out your stuff.

And don't forget about email marketing! I know, I know, you're probably thinking, "Email? Isn't that so 2005?" But let me tell ya, it's still one of the most powerful tools in your marketing arsenal. Think of it as your direct line to your customers.

Here's the deal: when someone buys from you, that's your chance to get their email. Use it! Send out newsletters about new products, special promotions, or even just a friendly hello. Keep it light and engaging. Maybe throw in a funny meme or two. You want your customers to look forward to your emails, not dread them like a Monday morning meeting.

Now, let's break this down into actionable steps:

1. Social Media Marketing
   - Choose the right platform: Instagram for visuals, Facebook for community building.
   - Post consistently: Aim for at least three times a week.
   - Engage with your audience: Reply to comments, ask questions, and create polls.
   - Use hashtags wisely: Research popular hashtags in your niche and include them in your posts.

2. Influencer Marketing
   - Research potential influencers: Use tools like BuzzSumo or Instagram's search function to find relevant influencers.
   - Reach out: Send a personalized message explaining why you think they'd love your product.
   - Track results: Monitor the engagement and sales that come from influencer partnerships.

3. Email Marketing

  - Build your list: Offer a discount for signing up or a freebie related to your niche.

  - Create engaging content: Mix product promotions with fun stories or tips.

  - Analyze your open rates: Use tools like Mailchimp to see what's working and what's not.

Now, let's get real for a second. Marketing isn't a one-size-fits-all deal. You gotta experiment and find what works for you. Maybe you'll discover that Instagram stories bring in more sales than Facebook posts, or that email newsletters get opened more on Wednesdays. The key is to stay flexible and adapt to what your audience responds to.

And here's a little secret: don't be afraid to get personal. Share your story! People love connecting with the human side of a brand. Maybe you started your dropshipping journey to pay off student loans or to escape the 9-to-5 grind. Whatever it is, let your audience in on your journey.

So, what's the takeaway here? Use social media to get your products in front of people, leverage influencers to expand your reach, and keep your customers engaged through email marketing. It's all about building relationships and creating a community around your brand.

Now go out there and get to marketing! Your $100 million business isn't gonna build itself, right?

Chapter 37

The Power of Automation

Let's talk about automation. Now, I know what you're thinking: "Automation? Sounds like something only robots can handle!" But hold your horses! Automation is not just for the Jetsons or the Terminator. It's your best buddy in the dropshipping world, and it's here to save your sanity.

Imagine you're juggling flaming torches while riding a unicycle. That's what running a dropshipping business can feel like without automation. You've got inventory to manage, orders to process, and a mountain of customer emails piling up like laundry on a Sunday. It's overwhelming, right? But here's the kicker: with the right automation tools, you can turn that chaotic circus into a well-oiled machine.

So, let's break it down.

1. Efficiency is Key

Automation tools can help you manage your store more efficiently. You've got tasks that can suck up hours of your day—like tracking inventory or processing orders. Why not let a tool handle that? It's like having a personal assistant who never takes a coffee break.

2. Task Automation

Think about the tasks you can automate:

Inventory Management: Keep your stock levels in check without lifting a finger. Tools like TradeGecko or Skubana can alert you when you're running low on popular items.

Order Processing: Once a customer clicks "buy," the last thing you want is to manually enter their info into your system. Tools like ShipStation or Oberlo can streamline this process, automatically sending order details to your suppliers.

Customer Emails: Remember those emails you meant to respond to but never did? Automation can handle that too! Use tools like Mailchimp or ActiveCampaign to send out order confirmations, shipping updates, and even promotional offers—all while you kick back and enjoy a cup of coffee.

3. Time-Saving Magic

Now, let's get to the good stuff: saving time. You're not just automating for the sake of it; you're doing it to reclaim your precious hours. With all that time saved, you can focus on growing your business. Think about it: what would you do with an extra 10 hours a week? Maybe you'd brainstorm new marketing strategies, explore new niches, or finally take that yoga class you've been putting off.

Here's a little personal anecdote for you. When I first started my dropshipping journey, I was a one-person show. I spent countless hours processing orders and responding to customer inquiries. It felt like I was running in circles, and honestly, I was about to throw in the towel. Then I discovered automation tools, and it was like a light bulb went off. Suddenly, I had time to strategize and innovate instead of just treading water.

But let's be real—automation isn't a magic wand. You've still got to set things up properly. It's like assembling IKEA furniture: it looks easy, but you might end up with a few extra screws if you're not careful.

Here are some practical tips to get you started with automation:
 Choose the Right Tools: Do your homework. Look for tools that integrate well with your existing systems. Read reviews, watch tutorials, and maybe even ask fellow dropshippers for their recommendations.

Start Small: Don't try to automate everything at once. Pick one or two tasks to automate and expand from there. It's like dipping your toe into a pool before cannonballing in.

Test and Adjust: Once you've set up your automation, monitor how it's working. Are there hiccups? Are customers getting their emails? Adjust as needed. Automation should make your life easier, not harder.

Now, let's address a common misconception: "Isn't automation impersonal?" Well, sure, it can feel that way if you let it. But here's the thing—automation doesn't mean you're throwing customer service out the window. It's about efficiency while still providing a personal touch.

Consider this: You can automate your emails, but you can also personalize them. Use your customer's name, recommend products based on their previous purchases, or send a handwritten thank-you note with their first order. It's all about balance.

As you embrace automation, you'll find that it opens up new opportunities. You can scale your business faster than ever. You're not bogged down by mundane tasks, so you can focus on expanding your product line or tapping into new markets. And that's where the magic happens!

Speaking of magic, let's talk about some tools that can help you automate your dropshipping business:

Zapier: This tool connects your favorite apps and automates workflows. You can set up Zaps to automatically add new customers to your email list or send order notifications to your team.

Shopify Flow: If you're using Shopify, this built-in tool allows you to automate tasks like customer segmentation and inventory management without any coding.

Gorgias: This customer service platform integrates with your store and automates responses to common inquiries. It's like having a virtual assistant who never gets tired of answering "Where's my order?"

Now, before I wrap this up, let's talk about some common fears around automation. You might be worried about losing the human touch or making mistakes. But remember, automation is a tool, not a replacement for your passion and creativity.

You're still the heart of your business. You're the one making decisions, crafting your brand story, and connecting with your customers. Automation just helps you do it more efficiently.

So, are you ready to embrace the power of automation? Are you ready to turn your dropshipping business into a well-oiled machine?

Here's your challenge: Take a moment to identify one task you can automate this week. It could be as simple as setting up an email sequence or integrating your order processing system.

Once you've done that, take a step back and see how much time you've freed up. You might just find that automation is the secret ingredient you've been missing.

In conclusion, automation is your ally in the dropshipping game. It's about working smarter, not harder. By implementing the right tools and strategies, you can save time, reduce stress, and focus on what truly matters: growing your business and enjoying the journey. So go ahead, unleash the power of automation, and watch your business soar!

Chapter 38

Understanding Global Markets

Alright, let's chat about something that's really changed the way we do business: the internet. I mean, it's not just a tool anymore; it's like a magic key that opens up a world of opportunities. Imagine being a kid who just scored a golden ticket to Willy Wonka's factory. But instead of chocolate rivers and candy trees, you've got a bustling marketplace filled with potential customers from every corner of the globe. You can sell to anyone, anywhere, at any time. It's pretty wild when you think about it. The world is your oyster, and you're holding the pearl. But hold on a second—just because you can sell globally doesn't mean you should just leap in without a solid game plan.

Let's break this down, shall we? First things first, you need to wrap your head around the fact that different countries have their own unique buying habits and preferences. What's flying off the shelves in the U.S. might totally tank in Japan. Ever tried to sell a meat pie in a country where veganism is the norm? Yeah, good luck with that! So, here's the deal: research is your best friend. You've gotta dive into the data—market reports, consumer behavior studies, even social media trends. The more you know, the better you can customize your offerings to fit what people actually want.

Here's a little nugget of wisdom for you: Google Trends is a fantastic tool for spotting what products are trending in various countries. It's like having a crystal ball for your business decisions! You can see what keywords people are searching for, which is super handy. And don't forget to poke around local forums or social media groups. You'll get some real, unfiltered insights straight from the horse's mouth. It's amazing how much you can learn just by listening to what people are saying.

Now, let's get into the nitty-gritty of making those global sales happen. Back in the day, if you wanted to sell to someone in another country, you'd need a degree in international finance or something. But now? It's as easy as pie. Seriously! There are online currency converters that'll help you figure out pricing in a snap. No more guesswork when it comes to pricing your products for international customers. That's a huge relief, right?

And let's not even get started on shipping—oh boy! Companies like DHL, FedEx, and UPS have made it so straightforward to send your products worldwide. You can even set up shipping calculators on your website, so customers know exactly how much they're paying for delivery. Transparency is key here, folks. Nobody likes surprises when it comes to shipping costs, especially when they're international. You want your customers to feel confident in their purchase, not wondering if they'll get hit with some crazy fees at checkout.

Now, let's keep it real—there are definitely challenges when it comes to navigating global markets. Customs regulations, tariffs, and taxes can feel like a maze sometimes. But don't let that scare you off! Just like you wouldn't run a marathon without training, don't jump into global selling without knowing the rules of the road. Research the regulations for the countries you want to sell to. Trust me, it'll save you a ton of headaches down the line.

And speaking of headaches, let's chat about customer preferences. It's not just about what they want to buy; it's also about how they want to buy it. Some cultures prefer to pay with credit cards, while others might lean toward cash on delivery. You've gotta cater to those preferences if you want to make sales.

A great example of this is the rise of mobile payments in Asia. If you're not offering options like Alipay or WeChat Pay, you might as well be selling ice to Eskimos. Seriously, you've got to make sure you're providing a variety of payment options that cater to your target market. It's all about making it as easy as possible for your customers to complete their purchase.

Here's a little exercise for you: take a moment to jot down the top three countries you're interested in selling to. Then, for each country, write down three unique buying habits or preferences you've discovered. This little exercise will help you stay focused and organized as you build your global strategy.

Now, let's take a step back and remember what this is all about. Understanding global markets isn't just about expanding your reach; it's about connecting with customers on a deeper level. You want them to feel like you really get them, like you understand their needs and desires. When they feel that connection, they're way more likely to hit that "buy" button.

So, let's recap a bit, shall we?

1. The internet opens doors to global sales.
2. Research is crucial for understanding different buying habits.

3. Use currency converters and international shipping options to simplify the process.

4. Know the regulations and customs for the countries you're targeting.

5. Cater to local payment preferences to increase sales.

Alright, now that we've covered the basics, let's dive a little deeper into some of these points.

Understanding Your Audience

First off, let's talk about understanding your audience. It's not just about knowing what they want to buy, but also understanding who they are as people. What are their values? What are their pain points? What makes them tick? Getting to know your audience on a personal level can help you craft marketing messages that resonate with them.

For instance, let's say you're selling eco-friendly products. In some countries, sustainability is a huge selling point, while in others, it might not even be on their radar. You'll want to tailor your messaging accordingly. Use storytelling to connect emotionally with your audience. Share stories about how your products are made, who makes them, and the positive impact they have on the environment. People love a good story, and it helps them feel more connected to your brand.

Localization is Key

Next up, let's chat about localization. This is a biggie when it comes to selling globally. It's not enough to just translate your website into another language. You've got to localize your content to fit the culture and customs of the market you're targeting. This means understanding local idioms, humor, and even colors that may have different meanings in different cultures.

For example, in some cultures, the color red is seen as lucky and prosperous, while in others, it might symbolize danger or warning. If you're running ads or designing your website, you'll want to keep these cultural nuances in mind. It's all about making your customers feel at home when they visit your site.

Building Trust

Now, let's talk about trust. When you're selling internationally, building trust with your customers is absolutely essential. They can't just pop into your store and check out your products in person, so you've got to find other ways to establish credibility.

One way to do this is through customer reviews and testimonials. Encourage your customers to leave reviews after they make a purchase. You can even reach out to influencers in your target market to review your products. Having a trusted figure vouch for your brand can go a long way in building trust with potential customers.

Another way to build trust is by offering a clear and easy return policy. If customers know they can return a product if it doesn't meet their expectations, they'll feel much more comfortable making a purchase. And remember, transparency is key. Be upfront about shipping times, costs, and any potential customs fees they might incur.

Marketing Strategies for Global Sales

Now that we've covered the basics, let's get into some marketing strategies for your global sales.

Social Media Marketing

Social media is a powerful tool for reaching global audiences. Each platform has its own unique audience, so you'll want to tailor your content accordingly. For instance, Instagram is great for visually-driven products, while LinkedIn might be better suited for B2B sales.

Don't be afraid to get creative with your social media campaigns. Use eye-catching visuals, engaging captions, and relevant hashtags to draw in your audience. And remember, engagement is key. Respond to comments, ask questions, and encourage your followers to share their experiences with your products.

Email Marketing

Email marketing is another effective way to reach your global audience. Create segmented email lists based on customer preferences, behaviors, and demographics. This way, you can send targeted emails that speak directly to their interests.

Consider offering exclusive discounts or promotions to your email subscribers. This not only incentivizes them to make a purchase but also helps you build a loyal customer base. And don't forget to personalize your emails! Use their names and tailor the content to fit their preferences.

Content Marketing

Content marketing is all about providing value to your audience. Create blog posts, videos, and infographics that educate and inform your customers about your products, industry trends, and other relevant topics.

This not only helps establish your brand as an authority in your field but also drives traffic to your website. Plus, when you provide valuable content, your audience is more likely to share it with their networks, expanding your reach even further.

Networking and Partnerships
Lastly, don't underestimate the power of networking and partnerships. Collaborate with other businesses or influencers in

your target market to reach a wider audience. This could be through joint promotions, giveaways, or even co-hosting events.

Building relationships with other businesses can also lead to valuable insights and advice. Don't be afraid to reach out and connect with others in your industry. You never know what opportunities might arise!

Wrapping It Up

So, there you have it—a deep dive into understanding global markets and how to navigate them successfully. It's all about doing your homework, understanding your audience, and being adaptable. The world is a big place, and there's a ton of potential out there just waiting for you to tap into it.

Remember, every expert was once a beginner. Don't be afraid to make mistakes along the way. Just learn from them, adjust your approach, and keep moving forward. Your $100 million business is out there, and you're more than capable of making it happen.

So, go on—get out there and start exploring those global markets. You've got this!

Chapter 39

Customer Service Excellence

Let's talk about customer service, shall we? I mean, it's the lifeblood of any business, especially in the dropshipping game. You want repeat customers, right? You want those glowing reviews that make you feel like a rock star. Well, providing excellent customer service can get you there faster than a cheetah on roller skates. Seriously, it's that important.

First off, let's get one thing straight: if you're not responding quickly to customer inquiries, you're playing a dangerous game. Customers today expect answers faster than a microwave can heat up leftovers. You know what I mean? When they shoot you a message, they want to feel like they matter. And guess what? They do! So, if you want to build trust, you've got to be on it. Quick responses can turn a potential disaster into a success story. It's like turning lemons into lemonade—sweet, refreshing, and oh-so-satisfying.

Now, let's dig a little deeper. You might be thinking, "But I'm just one person! How can I handle all these inquiries?" I hear you! That's where technology comes to the rescue. Consider using

Chatbots. These little digital helpers can assist with common questions 24/7. Picture it: while you're catching some Z's or binge-watching the latest series on Netflix, your Chatbot is out there answering questions like a champ. Talk about efficiency! Plus, it frees you up to focus on the bigger picture—growing your business and sipping your morning coffee in peace.

But hold on, let's not get ahead of ourselves. Before you go diving into the world of Chatbots, let's break down how to provide that excellent customer service that keeps folks coming back for more. Here's a quick list to get you started:

1. Be Responsive: Aim to respond to inquiries within a few hours. If you can't, set expectations. Let them know when they can expect a reply.

2. Be Helpful: Don't just answer questions—go above and beyond. If a customer asks about a product, give them all the juicy details. Share tips on how to use it or suggest complementary items. Make them feel like they're chatting with a friend, not just a salesperson.

3.   Personalize Your Responses: Use their name and reference previous interactions if possible. It's like adding a sprinkle of magic to your communication. Everyone loves a personal touch!

4.   Follow Up: After resolving an issue, follow up with the customer to ensure they're satisfied. It shows you care. Plus, it gives you a chance to ask for that coveted review!

5.   Gather Feedback: Don't be shy about asking for feedback. It's like having a cheat sheet for what you can improve. You can use surveys or simple follow-up emails to gauge customer satisfaction.

Now, let's talk about those positive reviews. They're like gold in the dropshipping world. When potential customers see glowing testimonials, they're more likely to trust you. Think of it as social proof. It's like when your friend recommends a restaurant, and you're suddenly all in. You want that same effect for your business.

So, how do you get those reviews? Here's the kicker: you have to ask for them! Don't assume customers will just leave a review because they had a good experience. Send a follow-up email after their purchase, thanking them and gently nudging them to share their thoughts. Maybe even offer a small discount on their next purchase as a thank-you. It's a win-win!

Let's not forget about the power of resolving issues. Every business faces hiccups—whether it's a delayed shipment or a product that didn't meet expectations. How you handle these situations can make or break your reputation. Here's a little secret: when a customer has a problem, they're looking for solutions, not excuses. So, take ownership and work to resolve the issue quickly. It's like being a superhero in their eyes. They'll appreciate your efforts, and who knows? You might turn a frustrated customer into a lifelong fan.

Now, I know what you're thinking. "But what if I mess up?" Here's the thing: everyone makes mistakes. It's how you respond that counts. If you own up to your errors and show genuine concern, you'll come out on top. It's like when you accidentally spill coffee on your friend's new shirt. You apologize, help clean it up, and maybe even buy them a new shirt. They'll appreciate your honesty and willingness to make things right.

And let's circle back to those Chatbots. I can't stress enough how handy they can be. Imagine a customer has a question at 2 AM. They're not going to wait until you wake up to get their answer. A

Chatbot can swoop in and provide instant assistance. It's like having a trusty sidekick who never sleeps. Just make sure your Chatbot is programmed with accurate information and a friendly tone. Nobody wants to chat with a robot that sounds like it just downed a gallon of cough syrup.

In conclusion, if you want to build a $100 million business through dropshipping, excellent customer service is non-negotiable. It's the secret sauce that can turn one-time buyers into loyal customers. Be responsive, be helpful, and don't shy away from using technology to your advantage. With a little effort and the right tools, you can create a customer service experience that's as smooth as butter on warm toast.

So, what's your next move? Start implementing these strategies today. And remember, every interaction is an opportunity to shine. Go out there and make your customers feel like rock stars!

Chapter 40

Analyzing Your Data

Tracking your sales and website traffic is like having a treasure map for your dropshipping business. You want to know what's working and what's tanking faster than a lead balloon. If you don't keep an eye on those numbers, you might as well be sailing blindfolded. And trust me, I've been there. I remember when I first started my dropshipping journey. I thought, "Hey, if I build it, they will come." Spoiler alert: they didn't. It wasn't until I started tracking my data that I realized my marketing efforts were about as effective as a screen door on a submarine.

So, let's dive into the nitty-gritty of analyzing your data. First off, you need to track your sales and website traffic. Think of it as the heartbeat of your business. You wouldn't ignore a weak pulse, right? You want to know what products are flying off the virtual shelves and which ones are gathering dust like that old treadmill in your garage. Use tools like Google Analytics to get the lowdown on customer behavior. It's like having a backstage pass to your audience's thoughts and actions. You'll see where they're coming from, how long they're sticking around, and what's making them click that "Buy Now" button.

Now, let's break this down into some actionable steps. Here's what you need to do:

1. Set Up Google Analytics: If you haven't done this yet, get on it! It's free, and it's like having a personal assistant that never sleeps. Go to Google Analytics, create an account, and follow the setup instructions. It'll take you about 30 minutes, but trust me, it's worth every second.

2. Track Key Metrics: Focus on metrics that matter. Look at your traffic sources, bounce rate, and conversion rate. If you see a high bounce rate, it's like a neon sign saying, "Fix your website!" Maybe your page load speed is slower than molasses in January, or your site's as confusing as a Rubik's cube.

3. Analyze Customer Behavior: Use the insights from Google Analytics to understand what your customers are doing. Are they spending more time on certain product pages? Are they abandoning their carts? This data is GOLD. Adjust your strategies based on

what you find. If people are dropping off at checkout, maybe your shipping costs are too high or the process is clunky.

4. Adjust Your Strategies: Once you've got the data, it's time to make some moves. If you find that a particular product isn't selling, consider changing your marketing approach or even dropping it altogether. On the flip side, if something's a hit, double down! Increase your ad spend on that product and watch the sales roll in.

5. Regularly Review Your Data: Make it a habit to check your analytics weekly or monthly. This isn't a "set it and forget it" situation. The e-commerce landscape is like a fast-moving river; if you're not paddling, you'll get swept away.

You might be wondering, "How does all this data crunching lead to increased sales and profits?" Great question! When you adjust your strategies based on data, you're not just throwing spaghetti at the wall to see what sticks. You're making informed decisions that lead to better customer experiences and, ultimately, more sales. For example, if your data shows that customers are more likely to buy during a certain time of day, you can time your marketing campaigns accordingly. It's all about being strategic and responsive.

Let's talk about a personal experience. I remember when I launched a new product line. Sales were sluggish, and I was starting to sweat. I dug into my analytics and discovered that most visitors were dropping off right before checkout. After some sleuthing, I realized my shipping options were confusing. I simplified the process and added a few more shipping choices. Boom! Sales shot up like a rocket. It was a game-changer.

But here's the kicker: data analysis isn't just for the big players. Whether you're running a one-person show or a small team, the insights you gain can lead to BIG changes. You don't need to be a data scientist to understand the basics. Just keep it simple and focus on the numbers that matter.

So, what tools can you use besides Google Analytics? There are plenty of options out there. For example, consider using Hotjar for heatmaps and user recordings. It's like peeking over your customers' shoulders to see how they interact with your site. You'll get to know what catches their eye and what makes them click away.

Another great tool is SEMrush. It's not just for SEO; it can help you analyze your competitors too. Want to know what keywords they're ranking for? Or how their traffic compares to yours? SEMrush can give you that intel, allowing you to fine-tune your strategy.

And let's not forget about social media analytics. Platforms like Facebook and Instagram provide insights into how your posts are performing. If a certain type of content is getting a lot of engagement, create more of it! Your audience is telling you what they want—listen to them!

In the end, analyzing your data is all about creating a feedback loop. You track, you analyze, you adjust, and then you repeat. It's like a dance—sometimes you lead, sometimes you follow, but the goal is to keep moving forward.

Now, I know this can sound overwhelming, but here's a little encouragement: start small. Pick one area to focus on, whether it's tracking your sales or analyzing customer behavior. Set aside a couple of hours each week to dive into the numbers. Before you know it, you'll be a data wizard, conjuring up strategies that lead to increased sales and profits.

So, let's wrap this up with a challenge. This week, I want you to track one key metric in your business. Maybe it's your conversion rate or your average order value. Write it down, analyze it, and come up with one actionable strategy based on what you find. You'll be amazed at what a little data can do for your business.

Remember, the more you know about your customers and your business, the better equipped you are to make smart decisions. Embrace the numbers, and let them guide you toward success. You've got this!

Chapter 41

Scaling Your Business

Alright, so you've reached that golden moment in your dropshipping adventure. You're not just treading water anymore; you're cruising on a wave of success! But now, here comes the big question: how do you scale your business? Trust me, this is where things get really exciting. But before you dive headfirst into the deep end, let's take a moment to chat about what scaling actually means and how you can do it without feeling overwhelmed.

First off, once you've found a bit of success, it's time to think about EXPANDING. I mean, why not? Think of it like being at a buffet—sure, you've got your favorite dish that you could eat every day, but isn't it tempting to try a little bit of everything? Just like that buffet, your business can offer a whole variety of products. The more options you throw into the mix, the more customers you'll attract.

When I first dipped my toes into the dropshipping pool, I was laser-focused on just a couple of products. I thought, "Hey, if it ain't broke, don't fix it." But then, I had this lightbulb moment. I realized I was missing out on a ton of potential customers who were looking for something different. Once I decided to expand my product line and explore a few more categories, my sales shot up like a rocket. Seriously, it felt like I flipped a switch and everything changed overnight.

Now, how do you figure out what to add to your lineup? Well, keep your ear to the ground—stay in the loop! Use tools like Google Trends or scroll through social media platforms to see what's hot right now. What are people buzzing about? What's trending? If you can tap into those conversations, you'll be way ahead of the game. And hey, don't forget about seasonal products! A little holiday cheer can do wonders for your sales.

Speaking of growing your business, let's chat about the workload. As your business takes off, so does your to-do list. It's like that time I thought I could handle making Thanksgiving dinner for the whole family all by myself. Spoiler alert: I ended up with a turkey disaster and a mountain of takeout menus. Don't be like me! Instead, consider bringing in some virtual assistants to help you manage the increased workload. They can take care of the nitty-gritty stuff, freeing up your time for the big-picture planning.

Think about it: you can delegate tasks like customer service, social media management, or even product research. There are platforms like Upwork and Fiverr where you can find skilled virtual assistants at prices that won't break the bank. I remember the first time I hired a VA; it felt like I'd just discovered a superpower. Suddenly, I had time to focus on scaling my business instead of getting bogged down in the day-to-day grind.

But hang on, there's more to this scaling thing! You've got to keep your eyes peeled for market trends. It's like being a hawk—always on the lookout for what's coming next. The e-commerce landscape is constantly shifting, and if you're not paying attention, you could find yourself left in the dust.

Make it a point to regularly check in on your competitors. What are they up to? What strategies are working for them? You don't have to copy them, but understanding their moves can give you some pretty valuable insights. Attend webinars, read industry blogs, and engage with online communities. Staying informed will help you adapt and pivot when necessary.

Here's a little exercise for you: carve out some time each week to research trends. Make it a habit! Grab a cup of coffee, settle in with your laptop, and dive into the latest news in your niche. You'll be amazed at how much you can learn in just a short amount of time.

Now, let's break this down into some actionable steps that you can start implementing right away.

First up, Expand Your Product Range: Take a moment to identify at least three new products or categories that you'd like to explore. Do a little research to see what the demand looks like and whether these products could be profitable for you.

Next, Hire Virtual Assistants: Create a list of tasks that you'd like to delegate. It could be anything from answering customer inquiries to managing your social media accounts. Then, start your search for virtual assistants who can help lighten your load.

And finally, Stay Ahead of Trends: Dedicate one hour each week to market research. Use tools like Google Trends, social media, and competitor analysis to gather insights. This little commitment can pay off big time.

Scaling your business is an exhilarating journey, and with the right strategies, you can take it to new heights. Just remember, it's all about being proactive and staying adaptable. Keep pushing forward, and who knows? You might just build that $100 million business you've been dreaming about!

So, are you ready to take the plunge? Let's roll up our sleeves and get to work!

Now, let's dive a bit deeper into each of these points. Because scaling isn't just about adding products or hiring help; it's about creating a sustainable and thriving business that you can be proud of.

When you think about expanding your product range, it's not just about throwing a bunch of random items into your store and hoping for the best. You want to be strategic about it. Think about your existing customer base—what do they love? What are they asking for? You can even send out a quick survey to your loyal customers to gather their feedback. This not only shows that you value their opinion but also gives you direct insight into what they're interested in.

And here's a little tip: don't be afraid to experiment. Maybe you've got a hunch that a certain product will do well. Test it out! Start with a small batch, see how it performs, and adjust your strategy based on the results. It's all part of the learning process, and sometimes the best ideas come from taking a leap of faith.

Now, let's chat about hiring virtual assistants. This is a game-changer. When I first started scaling my business, I was hesitant to let go of control. I thought, "No one can do it as well as I can!" But the truth is, once I let go of some of those tasks, I realized how much more I could accomplish. It's like shedding a heavy backpack after a long hike—you feel lighter and ready to tackle the next challenge.

When you're looking for virtual assistants, be clear about what you need. Create a detailed job description that outlines the tasks you want them to handle, the skills you're looking for, and any specific requirements. This will help you attract the right candidates. And don't forget to communicate! Set expectations early on and maintain an open line of communication. This way, you can ensure that everyone is on the same page and working towards the same goals.

Now, about keeping an eye on market trends—this is crucial. The e-commerce world is like a fast-moving river; if you're not paddling in the right direction, you might get swept away. Set aside some time each week to read industry news, follow thought leaders on social media, and engage with online communities. Join forums, participate in discussions, and don't be afraid to ask questions. The more you immerse yourself in the conversation, the more insights you'll gain.

And here's a little secret: don't just look at your own niche. Sometimes, inspiration can come from the most unexpected places. Look at what's happening in other industries. How are businesses adapting to changes? What innovative ideas are they implementing? You might just stumble upon a concept that you can adapt to your own business.

Let's not forget about the importance of customer feedback as you scale. Your customers are your best resource. Encourage them to leave reviews, share their experiences, and provide suggestions. Create a feedback loop where you actively seek out their opinions and use that information to improve your offerings. When customers see that you're listening and making changes based on their feedback, it builds trust and loyalty.

And speaking of loyalty, consider implementing a customer loyalty program. It's a fantastic way to reward your existing customers while also encouraging repeat business. You could offer discounts, exclusive access to new products, or even special promotions for loyal customers. This not only boosts your sales but also creates a community around your brand.

As you scale, don't forget about the power of storytelling. People connect with stories, and your brand has one to tell. Share your journey, your challenges, and your successes. Let your customers in on the behind-the-scenes action. This humanizes your brand and creates a deeper connection with your audience.

And, of course, let's not overlook the importance of branding as you expand. As you add new products and services, make sure your branding remains consistent. Your brand is more than just a logo; it's the feeling people get when they interact with your business. Keep that in mind as you grow, and ensure that everything from your website to your packaging reflects your brand's values and mission.

So, to wrap it all up, scaling your business is an exciting journey filled with opportunities. It's about expanding your product range, hiring the right help, staying on top of market trends, and building strong relationships with your customers. It's a lot to juggle, but with the right strategies and a proactive mindset, you can take your business to new heights.

Remember, it's not just about the numbers; it's about creating something meaningful. You're building a brand that resonates with people, and that's something to be proud of. So, are you ready to take the plunge? Let's roll up our sleeves and get to work! The sky's the limit, and your dreams are just waiting to be realized. Let's make it happen!

Chapter 42

Building a Brand

A strong brand identity can make or break your business. Think about it: when you hear "Nike," what pops into your head? Swoosh, right? Or maybe you think of "Just Do It." That's the power of a brand. It connects you with customers on a deeper level. You want your brand to evoke feelings, not just thoughts. You want people to feel something when they see your logo or hear your name. So, how do you build that kind of brand? Let's dive in.

First off, let's talk about consistency. Imagine you walk into a restaurant and the menu changes every time you visit. One day it's Italian, the next it's Mexican. Confusing, right? You'd probably walk out and never return. The same goes for your brand. Consistent branding across your website, social media, and packaging is essential. You want your customers to recognize you instantly. Use the same colors, fonts, and tone of voice everywhere. It's like wearing the same jersey for your favorite team—everyone knows who you're rooting for!

Here's a quick checklist to ensure your branding is consistent:

Logo: Is it the same on all platforms?

Color Scheme: Are you using the same colors across your website and social media?

Voice: Is your writing style consistent? Are you friendly, formal, or quirky?

Packaging: Does your product packaging match your brand's look and feel?

Now, let's shift gears a bit and talk about storytelling. You've probably heard the phrase, "Facts tell, stories sell." Well, it's true! People connect with stories. They want to know the "why" behind your brand. What inspired you to start this business? What challenges did you face? Share your journey. Let your audience in on your highs and lows.

For instance, I once had a friend who started a small coffee shop. She didn't just sell coffee; she shared her story about how she traveled to Ethiopia, fell in love with the coffee culture, and brought that passion back home. Customers weren't just buying coffee; they were buying a piece of her adventure. They felt connected to her, and that's what kept them coming back.

To create your brand story, consider these elements:

Origin: Where did your idea come from?

Challenges: What hurdles have you overcome?

Mission: What do you stand for? What's your brand's purpose?

Vision: Where do you see your brand going in the future?

Now, you might be wondering, "How do I even start telling my brand story?" Well, start by jotting down key moments in your journey. Don't overthink it! Just write. Once you have your notes, shape them into a narrative that feels authentic to you.

But wait, there's more! Engaging with your audience is crucial. Social media isn't just a platform for promotion; it's a place for conversation. Respond to comments, ask questions, and share user-generated content. Make your customers feel like they're part of your brand's story.

Here's a fun exercise: create a social media post asking your followers to share their experiences with your product. You might be surprised by the heartfelt stories they share. It's like building a community around your brand. And who doesn't want that?

Let's not forget about visual storytelling. Your visuals should complement your brand identity. Think about how you can use images, videos, and graphics to enhance your story. If you're selling fitness gear, show real people using your products in real-life situations. It's relatable and makes your brand feel more human.

Now, let's talk numbers. Research shows that consistent branding can increase revenue by up to 23%. That's a significant boost! If you want to tap into that potential, you need to prioritize your brand identity.

Here's a quick recap of actionable steps you can take to build your brand:

1. Define Your Brand Identity: What do you want your brand to represent?
2. Ensure Consistency: Use the same visuals and tone across all platforms.
3. Craft Your Brand Story: Share your journey and mission with your audience.

4. Engage with Your Customers: Build a community around your brand through social media.

5. Utilize Visuals: Use images and videos to enhance your storytelling.

Remember, building a brand isn't a sprint; it's a marathon. It takes time and effort. But trust me, the rewards are worth it. You're not just selling products; you're creating a brand that resonates with people.

So, what are you waiting for? Get out there and start building your brand! You've got this!

Chapter 43

Managing Finances: A Friendly Guide to Keeping Your Money in Check

Alright, let's chat about something that can feel like a mountain of paperwork: managing your finances. You know, keeping track of your income and expenses is a lot like cleaning your house. If you let it slide for too long, things get messy, and before you know it, you're drowning in a sea of receipts, bills, and that one pizza box you swear you threw away last week. Trust me, I learned this the hard way when I dove headfirst into my dropshipping adventure. I was so laser-focused on finding the perfect niche and crafting killer marketing strategies that I totally neglected my finances. Spoiler alert: it didn't end well. So, let's break this down and figure out how to keep your financial house in order, shall we?

First off, it's super important to realize that managing your finances isn't just about knowing how much cash is flowing into your account. Nope, it's also about understanding where that money is going. I mean, you wouldn't drive your car without checking how much gas is in the tank, right? Same deal with your business. So, let's dive into why tracking your income and expenses is absolutely crucial.

Financial Health: It's like looking in a mirror. You need to see the bigger picture. Are you actually making a profit, or are you just running in circles, feeling like a hamster on a wheel?

Budgeting: Knowing what you're spending allows you to create a budget that actually makes sense. This way, you can allocate funds to things that really matter—like that advertising campaign you've been dreaming about or, I don't know, a shiny new website design that doesn't look like it was made in 1995.

Decision Making: Good financial records are your best friends when it comes to making informed decisions. Thinking about scaling your business? You need to know if you can afford it.

Now, you might be sitting there thinking, "Okay, I get it. But how do I keep track of all this?" Well, let me introduce you to the magic of accounting software. Seriously, if you're not using one, you're totally missing out. There are so many tools out there that can make your life a whole lot easier. Here are a few that I've found super helpful:

QuickBooks: Think of this as the Swiss Army knife of accounting. It tracks your income, expenses, and even helps with invoicing. It's got a little bit of everything.

FreshBooks: This one's perfect if you need to send invoices. It's user-friendly and helps keep everything organized, so you won't lose track of who owes you money.

Wave: If you're looking for a free option, this is great for small businesses. It handles invoicing, accounting, and even receipt scanning.

The best part? Most of these tools can sync with your bank accounts. Imagine waking up to a neatly organized financial report instead of a mountain of receipts staring you down. Sounds dreamy, right?

Now, let's switch gears a bit and talk about something that can make your head spin faster than a tilt-a-whirl at the county fair: taxes and regulations. If you're planning to sell globally, you've got to be aware of the tax implications in different countries. Each country has its own set of rules, and trust me, you don't want to mess this up. Here's how to tackle this beast:

Research: Spend some time getting to know the tax laws in the countries you're selling to. It's like studying for a big exam, but way less fun.

Consult a Professional: If you can swing it, hire a tax pro who understands international regulations. It might cost you upfront, but it'll save you a headache down the line.

Stay Updated: Tax laws change, and you need to keep your finger on the pulse. Sign up for newsletters or follow relevant blogs to stay in the know.

I remember when I first started selling internationally. I thought, "How hard could it be?" Well, let me tell you, I was hit with unexpected fees and taxes that ate into my profits. It was a wake-up call. Now, I make it a point to stay informed about the financial regulations in every market I enter.

Alright, let's pivot back to the nitty-gritty of managing your finances. Here's a simple step-by-step guide to get you started on the right foot:

Set Up a Separate Business Account: Mixing personal and business finances is like trying to mix oil and water. They just don't go together. Open a separate account for your business to keep things clean and clear.

Track Everything: Use your accounting software to log every single transaction. I mean EVERY transaction. From that $5 ad spend to the $200 you dropped on a new product line, it all counts.

Review Regularly: Set a time each week or month to review your finances. This is like your financial check-up. Are you on track? Do you need to cut costs?

Plan for Taxes: Set aside a percentage of your income for taxes. It's way better to be prepared than to scramble when tax season rolls around.

Create a Budget: Outline your expected income and expenses. This will help you stay on track and avoid overspending.

Remember, managing your finances is a marathon, not a sprint. It takes time and discipline, but trust me, the payoff is totally worth it. You'll feel more in control, and your business will be healthier for it.

And hey, if you ever find yourself feeling overwhelmed, don't sweat it. We've all been there. Just take a deep breath and tackle one thing at a time. Start small, and before you know it, you'll have a solid grasp on your finances.

So, let's recap. Keeping track of your income and expenses isn't just a good idea; it's a necessity. Utilize the right tools, understand the regulations, and stay on top of your financial game. Your future self will thank you, trust me.

Now, if you're still with me, let's dig a little deeper. I want to share some personal stories and insights that might just resonate with you.

When I first started my dropshipping business, I was riding high on the thrill of entrepreneurship. It felt exhilarating, like standing at the edge of a diving board, ready to leap into the unknown. But as I got deeper into it, the reality of managing finances hit me like a ton of bricks. I remember sitting at my kitchen table one night, surrounded by a chaotic mess of invoices, receipts, and a growing sense of dread. My heart raced as I realized I had no idea how much I was actually making—or losing.

That's when I decided enough was enough. I took a step back and made a plan. I set up a separate business account, and I started using QuickBooks. At first, it felt like learning a new language. I fumbled around, unsure of what to do. But as the days turned into weeks, I started to get the hang of it. I could see my income and expenses laid out clearly, and it was like a fog was lifting.

I remember the first time I reviewed my finances and saw a profit. I was, well, kinda shocked. I had been so focused on the hustle that I hadn't taken the time to appreciate the progress I was making. That moment was a game-changer for me. It motivated me to keep pushing forward, to keep refining my strategies, and to keep my financial house in order.

And let me tell you, budgeting became my new best friend. I started setting aside money for taxes, which, believe me, saved me from some serious panic when tax season rolled around. I also learned to prioritize my spending. Instead of splurging on every shiny new tool that popped up on my radar, I focused on what would actually help my business grow. It's amazing how clarity can change your perspective.

As I continued to grow, I also realized the importance of staying informed. I made it a habit to read up on financial regulations and tax laws. I even found a few online communities where fellow entrepreneurs shared their experiences and tips. It was comforting to know I wasn't alone in this journey.

Now, I want to encourage you to take a moment and reflect on your own financial journey. Are you feeling overwhelmed? Or maybe you're just starting out and feeling a bit lost? That's totally okay. We all start somewhere, and it's perfectly normal to feel a little daunted by the whole thing. Just remember, you're not alone in this.

Take it one step at a time. Start by setting up that separate business account. Then, dive into tracking your expenses. It might feel tedious at first, but trust me, it'll pay off in the long run. And don't forget to celebrate those small victories. Every time you log a transaction or review your finances, give yourself a little pat on the back. You're building a solid foundation for your business.

As you continue on this journey, keep in mind that it's okay to ask for help. Whether it's hiring a professional or reaching out to fellow entrepreneurs, there's no shame in seeking guidance. We're all in this together, after all.

So, as we wrap this up, I just want to say: managing your finances doesn't have to be a daunting task. With the right tools, a little bit of knowledge, and a dash of determination, you can take control of your financial future. Your future self will be so grateful for the steps you take today.

Now go out there and make those numbers work for you! You've got this!

Chapter 44

Dealing with Challenges

Every business faces challenges, and let me tell ya, dropshipping is no exception. Think of it like a rollercoaster ride—there are thrilling highs, but also some gut-wrenching drops. If you're gonna navigate this wild ride, being prepared is your best bet. So, grab your helmet and let's dive into the nitty-gritty of overcoming those bumps in the road.

First off, let's talk about some common challenges you might encounter. Supplier delays? Yep, they happen. Imagine you've got a hot product that everyone wants, but your supplier decides to take a vacation. Not cool, right? Or how about product quality problems? You think you're selling the latest and greatest, but when it arrives at your customer's doorstep, it's more like "meh." And don't even get me started on customer complaints. They can feel like a swarm of angry bees buzzing around your head.

So, what do you do when these hiccups come your way? Here's a little secret: it's all about mindset. Instead of letting setbacks crush your spirit, think of them as opportunities to learn. Every time something goes wrong, you've got a chance to strengthen your business. It's like lifting weights; the more you struggle, the stronger you become.

Let's break this down with some practical tips to tackle these challenges head-on:

1. Create a Contingency Plan
    - Before you even start selling, map out potential problems. Think about what could go wrong and how you'll handle it. Having a plan in place is like having an umbrella on a cloudy day—you might not need it, but it's good to have just in case.

2. Communicate with Suppliers
    - Keep those lines of communication open. If you sense a delay, reach out to your supplier and ask for updates. Sometimes a little nudge can speed things along. Plus, it shows you're proactive and care about your business.

3. Set Realistic Expectations for Customers
    - If you know a product is delayed, don't leave your customers in the dark. Send them an email, give them a heads-up. Honesty builds trust, and trust is gold in the e-commerce world.

4. Invest in Quality Control

   - When sourcing products, always order samples first. It's like dating before marriage—make sure the product is as good as it looks online. If it's not up to snuff, find another supplier. Your reputation is on the line!

5. Learn from Complaints

   - Every complaint is a chance to improve. Take feedback seriously. If customers are unhappy about a specific issue, address it. Maybe it's a product defect or shipping time—whatever it is, use it to refine your processes.

Now, I know what you're thinking: "But what if I mess up?" Here's the deal—everyone messes up. Even the big shots. Take it from me, I've had my fair share of flops. I once launched a product that I thought was going to be a hit. Spoiler alert: it wasn't. I learned the hard way that just because you think something is cool doesn't mean your customers will.

After that experience, I started paying closer attention to market trends and customer feedback. I realized that setbacks aren't the end of the world; they're stepping stones to success. So, embrace the learning curve.

You might be wondering, "How do I actually learn from these setbacks?" Great question! Here's how you can turn those fumbles into fuel for growth:

Reflect on What Went Wrong

- After a setback, take a moment to analyze the situation. What could you have done differently? What steps can you take to ensure it doesn't happen again?

Document Your Experiences

- Keep a journal of challenges and solutions. This not only helps you remember what worked but also serves as a reference for the future. Plus, it's a great way to track your growth as an entrepreneur.

Seek Feedback from Peers

- Don't go it alone. Talk to other dropshippers or business owners. They've likely faced similar challenges and can offer valuable insights.

Stay Adaptable

- The business landscape is constantly changing. Be willing to pivot and adjust your strategies as needed. Flexibility is key in overcoming challenges.

To wrap it all up, dealing with challenges is part of the dropshipping game. Embrace the ride, learn from your experiences, and keep pushing forward. Remember, every setback is a setup for a comeback. So, gear up, stay focused, and let's conquer those challenges together. You've got this!

Chapter 45

Staying Ahead of Trends

Alright, let's dive into something that's become a real hot topic lately: staying ahead of trends in the e-commerce world. You know, the e-commerce landscape is a bit like a rollercoaster ride—one minute you're soaring high, feeling like a champ, and the next, you're plummeting down, maybe even upside down, holding on for dear life. If you want to make it in this wild ride, you've gotta keep your eyes wide open and your ears tuned in. Seriously, it's not just a "nice-to-have" anymore; it's a total must if you want to not just survive but actually thrive in this fast-paced world.

So, let's get into the nitty-gritty of how to keep your finger on the pulse of this industry. First off, think of following industry news and trends like you would follow your favorite celebrity on social media. You wouldn't miss a juicy update, right? Set up Google Alerts for key phrases that relate to dropshipping and e-commerce. This way, you'll be the first to know when something big drops. You want to be the one saying, "I saw that coming!" instead of playing catch-up like a kid trying to keep up with a game of tag.

But here's the thing—it's not just about reading articles and mindlessly scrolling through feeds. You need to dig a little deeper. Webinars and conferences? They're like treasure chests filled with valuable insights. Picture it as a treasure hunt where you can find those golden nuggets of wisdom that can really change the game for you. I remember my first e-commerce conference like it was yesterday. I was a bundle of nerves, pacing around like a cat in a room full of rocking chairs. But once I stepped inside, it was like a light bulb went off in my head. I soaked up the latest trends, rubbed elbows with industry leaders, and even forged connections that turned into partnerships. It was a game-changer for me.

Now, you might be wondering, "How do I find these events?" Well, websites like Eventbrite or Meetup are fantastic places to start. Just search for keywords like "dropshipping," "e-commerce," or "digital marketing," and you'll uncover a mix of local meetups and global conferences. And hey, if you can't make it to a physical event, don't sweat it! Many conferences now offer virtual attendance options. You can still soak up knowledge from the comfort of your couch— bonus points if you do it in your pajamas, right?

Networking is another crucial piece of the puzzle. When you attend these events, don't just sit there like a wallflower. Engage! Ask questions, share your experiences, and don't be afraid to show a little personality. People tend to remember those who stand out, and you want to be the one they can't forget. Think of it as building your personal brand. You're not just selling products; you're selling YOU.

But let's get real for a second—keeping up with trends can feel like trying to drink from a fire hose. It's overwhelming! To make it easier, create a system for yourself. Here's a quick tip: set aside a specific time each week to catch up on industry news. Maybe it's Sunday morning with a cup of coffee in hand or Friday afternoons as you wind down for the weekend. Whatever works for you, stick to it!

And don't forget about social media. Seriously, it's a goldmine. Follow industry leaders, join relevant groups, and jump into discussions. LinkedIn is a fantastic platform for professional networking, while Twitter can keep you updated on the latest buzz. Just remember, social media is a two-way street. Don't just consume; contribute! Share your insights, retweet valuable content, and engage with others. You'll build relationships and establish yourself as a thought leader before you know it.

Now, let's touch on something that's often overlooked: adaptability. The e-commerce world is like a game of chess—constantly changing, and you need to be ready to pivot at a moment's notice. What worked last year might not cut it this year. So, keep an open mind and be willing to experiment.

I had this one product that was flying off the shelves. I thought I had it all figured out, you know? But then, out of nowhere, a new competitor popped up with a similar product, and my sales took a nosedive. Instead of throwing in the towel, I took a step back, analyzed what went wrong, and adapted my strategy. I revamped my marketing, introduced new features, and even tweaked my pricing. It wasn't easy, but in the end, it paid off big time.

Here's a little exercise for you: take a moment to jot down the top three trends in e-commerce that you think could impact your business. Are there any emerging technologies, consumer behaviors, or market shifts you need to be aware of? Write them down and create a plan for how you can leverage these trends to your advantage.

Remember, staying ahead of trends isn't just about being reactive; it's about being PROACTIVE. Anticipate changes before they happen. Think of yourself as a trendsetter, not just a trend follower. When you can predict where the market is headed, you'll be in a prime position to capitalize on new opportunities.

In summary, staying ahead of trends in the e-commerce landscape is absolutely essential for success. Follow industry news, attend webinars and conferences, and network like a pro. Create a system for staying informed, engage on social media, and be adaptable to change. The world of dropshipping is full of surprises, but with the right mindset and strategies, you can navigate it like a champ.

So, what's your next move? Grab your notebook, set some time aside, and start researching those trends. You've got this!

Let's dive a bit deeper into some of these points, shall we? Because there's so much more to unpack when it comes to staying ahead in this ever-evolving e-commerce scene.

First, let's chat about the importance of understanding your audience. It's not just about knowing who they are; it's about really getting into their heads and hearts. What do they want? What keeps them up at night? What makes them tick? You've gotta think like a detective, piecing together clues from their behavior and preferences.

For instance, if you're selling fitness gear, it's not enough to know that your customers are into working out. You need to know what type of workouts they prefer—are they into yoga, CrossFit, or maybe they're training for a marathon? What are their pain points? Maybe they struggle to find gear that fits well or is affordable. The more you understand your audience, the better you can tailor your products and marketing strategies to meet their needs.

And speaking of marketing, let's talk about storytelling. People love stories—it's in our DNA. When you share the story behind your brand or your products, you create an emotional connection with your audience. It's not just about selling; it's about creating a narrative that resonates with them.

Think about it: when you buy a product, you're not just purchasing an item; you're buying into a story, a lifestyle, or a solution to a problem. So, don't be shy! Share your journey, your challenges, and your victories. Maybe you started your e-commerce business in your garage, or you faced setbacks that made you question everything. Those stories are powerful—they can inspire others and create a loyal customer base.

Now, let's pivot a bit and talk about the role of technology in e-commerce. It's a game-changer, folks. From AI chatbots that provide customer service 24/7 to analytics tools that help you understand your sales patterns, technology can streamline your operations and give you insights that were unimaginable just a few years ago.

Take the time to explore new tools and platforms that can enhance your business. Maybe it's an inventory management system that helps you keep track of stock levels, or a social media scheduling tool that saves you hours each week. Embrace the tech that can make your life easier and your business more efficient.

And let's not forget about the importance of customer feedback. This is gold! Encourage your customers to leave reviews and share their experiences. It's not just about collecting testimonials; it's about gaining valuable insights that can help you improve your products and services.

I remember launching a new product and thinking it was perfect. But after getting some feedback, I realized there were a few tweaks I could make to enhance the user experience. I listened to my customers, made those changes, and saw a significant boost in sales. It's all about being open to feedback and willing to make adjustments.

Alright, let's shift gears again and talk about the importance of building a community around your brand. This goes hand-in-hand with networking but takes it a step further. You want your customers to feel like they're part of something bigger. Create a space where they can connect with each other, share their experiences, and engage with your brand.

Consider starting a Facebook group or an online forum where your customers can chat, ask questions, and share tips. This not only fosters loyalty but also gives you direct access to their thoughts and ideas. Plus, it creates a sense of belonging—people love being part of a community.

And finally, let's wrap this up with a reminder about the power of perseverance. The e-commerce journey isn't always smooth sailing. There will be bumps along the way—maybe a product flops, or you face unexpected challenges. But don't let that discourage you. Every setback is an opportunity to learn and grow.

I've had my fair share of challenges, and I can tell you, the key is to stay resilient. Keep pushing forward, keep adapting, and keep learning. Surround yourself with supportive people who lift you up and inspire you to keep going.

So, as you embark on your journey to stay ahead of trends in e-commerce, remember to stay curious, stay engaged, and most importantly, stay true to yourself. You've got what it takes to make waves in this industry.

Now, go grab that notebook and start jotting down your ideas. Research those trends, connect with others, and don't be afraid to put yourself out there. You're not just in this to play the game; you're here to change it. So, what are you waiting for? Let's get to work!

Chapter 46

Research Your Suppliers

Let's take a moment to chat about the future of dropshipping. Spoiler alert: it's not just about slapping products on a website and waiting for the cash to roll in. Nope, not even close! The dropshipping industry is evolving faster than a cat on a hot tin roof. Seriously, new technologies are popping up everywhere, and customer expectations are shifting like the weather in the Midwest— one minute it's sunny, the next it's snowing. So, what does this mean for you, the aspiring dropshipper? Buckle up, because we're diving deep into the trends that are reshaping the game.

First off, let's talk tech. You've probably heard the buzz about AI, machine learning, and all that jazz. But what does it mean for dropshipping? Well, think about it this way: if you're still using the same old methods to run your business, you might as well be trying to send a text on a rotary phone. Seriously, who does that anymore? Embracing new technologies can streamline your operations, making your business not just faster but smarter. Imagine using chatbots to handle customer inquiries or predictive analytics to forecast trends. It's like having a crystal ball that tells you what your customers want before they even know it themselves. How cool is that?

Now, let's shift gears and talk about something that's becoming more important than a good cup of coffee in the morning—sustainability and ethical sourcing. Consumers today are more aware than ever of where their products come from. They're not just looking for the cheapest option; they want to know if their purchases are making the world a better place. This means you need to be on your A-game when it comes to sourcing your products. If you're still getting your items from questionable suppliers, you're gonna have a tough time attracting the modern consumer.

Here's a little story for you: I once bought this fancy coffee maker that promised the world but came from a factory with a questionable reputation. I loved that machine, but every time I used it, I felt a twinge of guilt. I mean, who wants to sip their morning brew while feeling like they're contributing to a problem? Now, imagine if I had known that the maker sourced their materials sustainably. I'd be sipping my coffee guilt-free, right? That's the power of ethical sourcing. It builds trust and loyalty.

So, how do you incorporate sustainability into your dropshipping business? Here are a few tips to get you started:

1. Research Your Suppliers: Don't just take their word for it. Dig into their practices. Are they using sustainable materials? Do they pay fair wages?
2. Choose Eco-Friendly Products: Look for items that are biodegradable, recyclable, or made from renewable resources.
3. Be Transparent: Share your sourcing story with your customers. Let them know you care about the planet.

Now, let's circle back to innovation. Embracing new ideas isn't just a nice-to-have; it's a MUST if you want to thrive in the global market. Think about the brands that have taken off in recent years. They didn't just follow the crowd; they created their own path. They leveraged technology, tapped into customer desires, and created experiences that people can't resist.

Here's where you come in. How can you be that innovative brand? Start by asking yourself a few questions:

- What gaps do you see in the market?

- How can you leverage technology to solve customer pain points?

- What unique experiences can you offer that set you apart?

Let's break it down with a few actionable steps:

1.   Stay Informed: Keep your finger on the pulse of industry trends. Subscribe to newsletters, join forums, and follow thought leaders in the dropshipping space.
2.   Experiment: Don't be afraid to try new things. Test different marketing strategies, product lines, and customer engagement tactics.
3.   Solicit Feedback: Your customers are your best source of information. Ask them what they like, what they don't, and what they wish you'd offer.

Now, I know what you might be thinking: "This all sounds great, but how do I actually implement it?" Here's the thing—don't let overwhelm stop you in your tracks. Start small. Pick one area to focus on, whether it's sustainability, technology, or innovation, and dive in.

For instance, if you choose to focus on sustainability, start by revamping your product line. Identify a few suppliers that align with your values and test their products. Once you've got that down, you can move on to other areas.

And remember, the future is all about adaptability. The dropshipping landscape is changing, and if you want to stay ahead, you need to be willing to pivot. Think of it like a dance—sometimes you lead, sometimes you follow, but you always keep moving.

In conclusion, the future of dropshipping is bright, but it's not without its challenges. By embracing new technologies, prioritizing sustainability, and fostering innovation, you can position your business for long-term success.

So, what's the takeaway? Get ready to roll up your sleeves and dive into the future. It's time to build a dropshipping empire that not only makes you money but also makes a positive impact on the world. Now, go on and get started—you've got this!

Alright, let's dig a little deeper into this whole dropshipping thing, shall we? You see, the future isn't just about keeping up with trends; it's about anticipating them. Think of it like surfing. You don't just want to catch the wave—you want to ride it all the way to the shore.

So, what are some of the waves you should be looking out for? For starters, let's chat about the rise of personalization. Today's consumers crave a tailored experience. They want to feel like you get them—like you know their likes, dislikes, and preferences. It's not enough to just throw a bunch of products at them and hope something sticks.

Imagine walking into a coffee shop where the barista knows your name and your usual order. That's the kind of connection people are looking for. You can create that same vibe in your dropshipping business by leveraging data. Use analytics to understand customer behavior, and then personalize their shopping experience.

For example, if someone frequently buys eco-friendly products, why not send them recommendations for similar items? Or maybe you could offer them a discount on their next purchase of a product they love. Little touches like these can make a world of difference and keep customers coming back for more.

Speaking of keeping customers engaged, let's talk about the importance of storytelling. People love a good story—it's in our DNA. We connect with narratives, and they help us relate to brands on a deeper level. So, don't just sell products; share the story behind them.

Take a moment to think about the brands you love. Chances are, there's a story behind why you're loyal to them. Maybe it's a mission-driven company that gives back to the community or a brand that started in someone's garage and grew into a global phenomenon. Whatever it is, share your journey with your customers. Let them in on the behind-the-scenes stuff.

For instance, if you're dropshipping handmade items from artisans, tell the story of those artisans. Share their backgrounds, their crafts, and what makes their products special. This not only builds a connection with your audience but also gives them a reason to choose you over competitors.

Now, let's not forget about the power of social media. It's not just a platform for cat videos and vacation photos; it's a goldmine for dropshippers. Social media allows you to connect with your audience in real-time, engage with them, and build a community around your brand.

Consider using platforms like Instagram or TikTok to showcase your products in action. Create engaging content that resonates with your target audience. Maybe it's a fun unboxing video, a tutorial on how to use your product, or even a behind-the-scenes look at your operations. The more authentic and relatable you are, the more likely people will want to engage with your brand.

And let's not forget about influencer marketing. Collaborating with influencers who align with your brand values can help you reach a wider audience. Just make sure they genuinely connect with your products. Authenticity is key here—consumers can sniff out inauthenticity from a mile away.

Now, let's pivot back to technology for a moment. As much as we love the personal touch, we can't ignore the role that tech plays in dropshipping. Automation is your friend. It can save you time and help you focus on the things that matter most—like growing your business and connecting with your customers.

Consider using tools that automate your inventory management, order processing, and customer communication. This way, you can spend less time on the nitty-gritty and more time on the big picture. Plus, automation helps reduce human error, which is always a win.

And while we're on the subject of tech, let's talk about the importance of mobile optimization. More and more people are shopping on their phones these days. If your website isn't mobile-friendly, you're missing out on a huge chunk of potential customers. Make sure your site is easy to navigate on a smaller screen, and consider offering mobile-exclusive deals to entice shoppers.

Alright, let's take a breather for a second. I know this is a lot to digest, but trust me, it's all worth it. The future of dropshipping is filled with opportunities, but it's up to you to seize them.

So, let's recap some key takeaways. First, embrace technology. Use AI, Chatbots, and analytics to streamline your operations and personalize the customer experience. Second, prioritize sustainability and ethical sourcing. Consumers want to support brands that align with their values, so make sure you're sourcing responsibly. Third, focus on storytelling and building a community around your brand. Share your journey, connect with your audience, and let them in on the behind-the-scenes magic.

And finally, don't forget about the importance of adaptability. The dropshipping landscape is ever-changing, and being able to pivot and adjust your strategies will set you apart from the competition.

Now, go on and get started! The future of dropshipping is waiting for you, and it's time to make your mark. Whether you're just starting out or looking to take your existing business to the next level, remember that you've got the tools and knowledge to succeed. So roll up those sleeves, put on your entrepreneurial hat, and dive headfirst into this exciting journey. You've got this!

Reference

Understanding Global Markets & Economic Trends

Friedman, Thomas L. The World Is Flat: A Brief History of the Twenty-first Century. Farrar, Straus and Giroux, 2005.

Ghemawat, Pankaj. World 3.0: Global Prosperity and How to Achieve It. Harvard Business Review Press, 2011.

McKinsey Global Institute. "Global flows: The ties that bind in an interconnected world." McKinsey & Company, 2022.

E-Commerce & The Digital Buyer Journey

Chaffey, Dave. "The E-commerce Growth Trend." Smart Insights, 2023.

KPMG. "The truth about online consumers." KPMG International, 2017.

Edelman, David C. "Branding in the Digital Age: You're Spending Your Money in All the Wrong Places." Harvard Business Review, 2010.

Understanding Local Customs & Cultural Barriers

Erin Meyer. The Culture Map: Breaking Through the Invisible Boundaries of Global Business. PublicAffairs, 2014.

Hofstede Insights. "National Culture." https://www.hofstede-insights.com

Sustainability & Ethical Buying

Elkington, John. Cannibals with Forks: The Triple Bottom Line of 21st Century Business. Capstone, 1999.

NielsenIQ. "Sustainable shoppers buy the change they wish to see in the world." NielsenIQ, 2023.

Customer Feedback & Personalization

Reichheld, Fred. The Ultimate Question 2.0: How Net Promoter Companies Thrive in a Customer-Driven World. Harvard Business Review Press, 2011.

Pine II, B. Joseph, and James H. Gilmore. The Experience Economy: Competing for Customer Time, Attention, and Money. Harvard Business Review Press, 2019.

Branding, Marketing & Buyer Behavior

Kotler, Philip, and Kevin Lane Keller. Marketing Management. Pearson Education, multiple editions.

Godin, Seth. Purple Cow: Transform Your Business by Being Remarkable. Portfolio, 2003.

HubSpot. "The State of Marketing Report." HubSpot Research, 2023.

Logistics, Tech & Supply Chain

Christopher, Martin. Logistics & Supply Chain Management. Pearson UK, 2016.

World Economic Forum. "The impact of technology on supply chains." WEF Reports, 2020.

Regulations & Global Compliance

Deloitte. "Global Regulatory Outlook." Deloitte Insights, 2023.

OECD. "International Regulatory Co-operation." Organisation for Economic Co-operation and Development, 2021.

Business Strategy & Scaling

Osterwalder, Alexander and Yves Pigneur. Business Model Generation. Wiley, 2010.

Christensen, Clayton M. The Innovator's Dilemma: When New Technologies Cause Great Firms to Fail. Harvard Business Review Press, 1997.

Harvard Business Review. "How to Build a Billion-Dollar Business." HBR.org, various authors, 2019–2024.

Success Stories & Case Studies

Forbes. "The World's Most Valuable Brands." Forbes Reports, annually.

CB Insights. "How 100 Startups Scaled to $1 Billion: Growth Lessons from Unicorns." CB Insights, 2023.

Y Combinator Blog. "Startup Lessons & Stories." https://www.ycombinator.com/blog

Metrics, KPIs & Growth

Lean Analytics by Alistair Croll and Benjamin Yoskovitz. Lean Analytics: Use Data to Build a Better Startup Faster. O'Reilly Media, 2013.

McKinsey & Company. "Measuring What Matters in Customer Experience." McKinsey Insights, 2020.

About the Author

Author: Harib Shaqsy.

He is the author of the best seller book "Hard Work Can Keep You Poor." In his book, Harib feels that most people are over working and over stressed unnecessarily, because, they believe that working hard is the only way to survive, be paid more and become richer, he explains why this is not true in his book.

You can also check some of Harib's work available in bookshops and online.

Visit website: http://haribshaqsy.com